PRAISE FOR *THE GROWTH DILEMMA*

"Ami Kassar makes *The Growth Dilemma* a great tool for entrepreneurs, turning a challenging subject into an easy read. Ami coaches each of us to understand our risk profile and our business outlook, combine those traits with facts and circumstances of our businesses, use that knowledge to quantify our needs for capital, and identify the most logical sources of capital for our specific situations. The stories he shares about real-life entrepreneurs makes it all relatable and really connects the dots."

—**Fran Tarkenton,** Founder and CEO of GoSmallBiz.com
and NFL Hall of Fame Quarterback

"First comes business strategy, then comes financial strategy. Money borrowed from oneself, or from investors, or from financial entities, or from all of the above is the oxygen needed for the business strategy. But before that come these questions: How big can my company get? . . . How big should my company get?. . . And how big do I want my company to get? Ami Kassar's book, rich with examples, will help entrepreneurs think deeply about the answers to these questions."

—**Lonnie Martin,** Chair of Vistage International

"My late father often liked to say, 'Growth is the single biggest cause of business failure.' The challenge of navigating the growth of a business is, for many business owners, a new experience that can often lead to financial disaster in spite of growing sales. In *The Growth Dilemma,* Ami Kassar helps to explain one of the biggest growth challenges facing any business owner—how to finance growth. Kassar weaves together the wisdom he has gained by building MultiFunding into an industry leader with stories and examples that bring the growth challenges facing business owners to life. This book is a must-read for any business owner who is experiencing the challenges of growth or who is contemplating impending growth in their business."

—**Jeff Cornwall,** Jack C. Massey Chair and Professor of
Entrepreneurship at Belmont University

The

GROWTH
DILEMMA

Determining Your Entrepreneurial Type
to Find Your Financing Comfort Zone

AMI KASSAR

AN INC.
ORIGINAL

An Inc. Original
New York, New York
www.inc.com

This work is being published under the An Inc. Original imprint by an exclusive arrangement with Inc. Magazine. Inc. Magazine and the Inc. logo are registered trademarks of Mansueto Ventures, LLC. The An Inc. Original logo is a wholly owned trademark of Mansueto Ventures, LLC.

Distributed by River Grove Books

Design and composition by Greenleaf Book Group
Cover design by Greenleaf Book Group
Cover image: Used under license from Shutterstock.com/By Who is Danny

Publisher's Cataloging-in-Publication data is available.

Print ISBN: 978-1-63299-162-1

eBook ISBN: 978-1-63299-163-8

First Edition

In honor of my dad, whose decade-long battle against colon cancer makes entrepreneurship feel easy.

Contents

Foreword ix

A Tale of Three FishPreneurs. xv

Introduction 1

Chapter 1: The Million-Dollar Question 9

Chapter 2: 100 Percenters vs. Safety Netters 17

Chapter 3: What Does Money Have to Do with It? 31

Chapter 4: Are You a Tortoise or a Hare?. 37

Chapter 5: Where Are You in Your Business Journey? . . .51

Chapter 6: What Is Your Risk Tolerance?. 69

Chapter 7: What Are Your Growth Aspirations? 87

Chapter 8: Should You Get a Loan to Grow?. 97

Chapter 9: Valuable Lessons in the Hunt for Money . . . 109

Chapter 10: Family Business/Partnerships 133

Conclusion: Finding Your Financing Comfort Zone . . . 141

Acknowledgments 149

Index 151

About the Author 159

Foreword

Like Ami Kassar, I came to entrepreneurship after trying other things. Like Ami, I first needed to get canned from a giant corporation (in my case, CBS). I landed at a little, entrepreneurial media company, Inc., that for 40 years had been single-mindedly writing about and offering advice to entrepreneurs. Like Ami, I came to regard helping entrepreneurs as more than a job. It is a calling.

For me, the awakening arrived a few years ago when I came across the story of an entrepreneur named Hil Davis (in *Inc.* magazine—where else?). Davis is the co-founder of an online clothing company called J. Hilburn. I had just become the editor of *Inc.*, and the article had been written before I arrived. I didn't know it was coming.

To understand why a story about an entrepreneur should have such an effect on me, it helps to know where I had come from.

Before *Inc.,* I had mostly covered Wall Street and personal finance for a number of big media companies, including Time Warner and CBS. So I spent a lot of time with Wall Street-ers. They tended to be quite intelligent, impeccably well-dressed, and almost always scandalously overpaid. But for all the smart people I met on that beat, and all the personal riches they piled up, it never struck me that they were making the world a better place.

So back to Hil Davis. Like me, he had left the Wall Street arena to do what he was meant to do. In his case, that was launching a business. Davis' vision was to create, more or less, the Warby Parker of custom tailored shirts. Rather than maintain a chain of physical stores, J. Hilburn went virtual. If you wanted to buy, the company would dispatch "stylists" to your house who would take measurements and consult on your order. Otherwise, almost all transactions were online. That would allow J. Hilburn to offer top-quality fitted shirts at a fraction of the brick-and-mortar price.

Or so Davis thought. As often happens in the startup world, things did not go as planned. Davis learned that his Chinese vendors had lied about the quality of their material and their manufacturing. His returns soared, and J. Hilburn's sales and reputation plummeted. Davis had put his personal net worth on the line to build J. Hilburn, and the company's troubles were starting to hit home. The bank foreclosed on his home, and he had to move his family into an apartment. Then his children's school called to say that if he didn't pay the arrears in their tuition, his kids would be kicked out.

Around that time, Wall Street came calling. Davis' old boss wanted him back and offered what's called a "three-by-three" contract: $3 million and guaranteed employment for three years. Davis thought about the straits he found himself and his family in. He talked the offer over with his wife.

And he said no.

Wow. At that point, I realized that, at *Inc.*, I was in a whole new game. I was no longer covering the cuff-linked elites who merely bankrolled the economy. I was now covering the people who built it: entrepreneurs. People like Hil Davis, who have the daring to start from scratch and build something great where nothing had existed before, and who had the stamina to stick with their dream even when it looked like they had lost. *Inc.* was a huge upgrade from where I had worked. Entrepreneurs like Davis are the engine of the free enterprise system, and telling their stories and offering them advice a) would be a lot more fun than writing about Wall Street, and b) to the extent that we at *Inc.* truly helped entrepreneurs, might actually contribute to making the world a little better.

(By the way, J. Hilburn survived Hil Davis' shoot-the-moon gamble. Investors came through at the last minute, the quality control issues were solved, and, as of this writing, the company is motoring along in its Dallas headquarters, although Davis is no longer with them.)

Not every entrepreneur is a growth-getter like Davis. Ami might characterize him as "risk-flexible" and an "aggressive stretcher," and as you'll see from the case studies that Ami introduces in *The Growth Dilemma,* Davis' toes-over-the-precipice business style isn't the only way to go. But at any level, eschewing conventional employment to start your own company takes guts. And without people with guts, free enterprise shrivels.

Virtually everyone now recognizes that entrepreneurs make an outsize contribution to the economy, but few understand just how oversized. At *Inc.,* we do, to some degree, thanks to our annual Inc. 5000, a listing of the fastest-growing private companies in America. To qualify for that listing, applicants actually tell us their revenues—which many entrepreneurs are otherwise reluctant to tell anyone—and that gives us a unique insight into fast-growing entrepreneurs' true contributions.

The scale is breathtaking: The average company in the 2017 Inc. 5000, for example, grew about 40 times faster than the U.S. economy as a whole over the previous three years. 40 times! Collectively, those 5000 companies had revenues of about $206 billion last year; that would make these 5000 small companies larger than the GDP of 27 states. And here's the kicker: Those 5000 companies accounted for fully half of all net US job growth since 2013.

Such companies can't do any of that without financing, however. If all you know about entrepreneur funding was what you learned by watching *Shark Tank* or CNBC, you'd imagine that all financing required equity and venture capital. But that's not so. Most Inc. 5000 founders started with money from their own savings, or their family's. And when they did raise capital, they first went to the bank or even their credit cards. Only about 25% received equity funding from venture capitalists or angels. Small businesses need financing, but overwhelmingly—even among the fastest-growing small businesses, like the Inc. 5000—that financing is built on credit.

That's why *The Growth Dilemma* is such a tremendously useful book. The variety and complexity of loans can be bewildering, the terms hard to grasp. The entry of a whole new category of online, algorithm-based lenders only complicates your choices further. And not every type of loan is right for every kind of entrepreneur at every stage of the entrepreneurial journey. As Ami points out in the pages to follow, at least half the job of discerning the right course in financing is understanding who you are, grasping where your business is right now, and forecasting where you would like it to go.

At *Inc.,* we spend a lot of time doing business with people who want to sell something to our audience of entrepreneurs. As you might imagine from the paragraphs above, I feel quite protective of that audience. I believe that, as entrepreneurs, they are the heroes of the free enterprise. As a result, I wouldn't give a platform to address them to just anyone.

But Ami is one of the good guys in the business. Ami knows the lending landscape intimately. Just as important, he knows the entrepreneurial mind equally well. I can't think of anyone more qualified to guide you through the process of matching your personality and business goals with the right source of capital. He has proven his credentials again and again with his column on Inc.com and his appearances at *Inc.* conferences. I trust him, and after reading his book, you'll see why.

I'm guessing that you picked up this book because you know that your business can benefit from a capital infusion and you are not quite sure where your comfort zone lies in the capital markets. After all, you didn't become an entrepreneur because you already knew all there is to know about financing a business. You launched because you have a dream—to build a great business, with all the

risk and responsibility that implies—and you need capital to realize that dream. If so, you've come to the right place. With Ami
Kassar, your dream is in good hands.

Eric Schurenberg
President and Editor-in-Chief, *Inc.*
Nov. 24, 2017

A Tale of Three FishPreneurs

Have you ever met an entrepreneur who is happy with their lot? Most entrepreneurs I work with are always pushing for their companies to grow and get bigger. At the same time, they struggle with decisions about how big they want to become, how much money to reinvest, and how to go about it. They want more, but they're not sure how to think about the problems, obligations, and risk that often come with growth. This is what I call the *growth dilemma*.

Perhaps a tale will help illustrate the point.

Three friends grew up in a small coastal fishing town. As they embarked upon their fishing careers, they didn't forget their roots; but each one tackled the world differently.

One FishPreneur stayed in town. His life didn't change much.

He took his pole to the waterfront every day and caught a few fish. He sold them to a store and made a modest living. He made enough to live a safe and peaceful life.

The second FishPreneur wanted more. And while she started on the same path as the first FishPreneur, she attended a business class and wrote a business plan to secure a loan to buy a fleet of five boats. She hired employees and had to keep them motivated and paid to keep her boats on the water so that she could make her debt payments. As the business grew, she needed an office manager to keep track of the paperwork and manage her fleet. She had to rent a small yard to store her boats. She enjoyed her life but didn't enjoy having to spend more time administering and less time on the water.

The third FishPreneur was the most restless. He also bought a few boats and had a crew. But he wanted more. He wanted to raise more money and open a fish-packaging plant. He couldn't do it with debt alone, so he took on some investors to fund the packaging plant. He had a board of directors to worry about and a lot of pressure to keep them happy and make the returns they wanted. He traveled a lot and had cash flow worries as he grew his business. Sadly, he never got out on the water anymore.

The contrasts in the lives of these three FishPreneurs illustrate the choices entrepreneurs make as they decide how to build their businesses. Each FishPreneur decided to grow their business to a different size and complexity. They sorted through their own growth dilemmas and made their choices.

Based on their decisions, they picked different *financing comfort zones* with various levels of risk and different financing instruments appropriate to the type and size of businesses they built.

REFLECTION

Have you sorted through your growth dilemmas in your business? Are you comfortable with your business size and growth plans? Are you in your financing comfort zone—have you found a financing structure that you are comfortable with to help you reach your goals?

My hope is that this book will help you think through these difficult and very personal decisions.

Introduction

A LITTLE BIT ABOUT MYSELF

I am a lifelong entrepreneur. I've worked at several companies, helped turn one around, and even started one that ultimately went belly-up. (It was an internet shopping site about fifteen years before people actually shopped on the internet.) I worked full time while I earned my MBA at the University of Southern California, because I didn't want to miss out on gaining real-world experience as I pored over those B-School case studies.

In 2010, I lost my big, fat corporate job at a company that was the largest issuer of credit cards to small businesses in the United States. I thought I was going to retire there. We had a thousand employees and a million customers. We helped countless entrepreneurs obtain credit—and achieve subsequent business growth—that they had never dreamed would be possible. I loved my job because I loved helping those entrepreneurs achieve their dreams.

And then we blew up in the great recession.

After months of wrangling and layoffs, the bankruptcy trustees fired me on a Friday. On my way home, I stopped at my bank and opened a new business account with a check from my home-equity line of credit. The full amount. Thankfully, I had opened that line of credit years before.

I tell the story about my home-equity line of credit because I understand what it means to be an entrepreneur and take a risk. It's also an important lesson that the best time to get a loan is when you don't need one. I could never have gotten a home-equity line of credit after that Friday when I no longer had a job.

MULTIFUNDING

The next day, on Saturday, I started my company, MultiFunding, which I'd been thinking about for many months.

I wanted to create an entrepreneurial company that would help entrepreneurs grow their businesses using financing methods they may not have known about or thought possible. I'd seen the need for a company like this, and I decided it was time to try it. And no, I didn't let my past failure (the internet-shopping venture) hold me back.

My company started out subletting a room in an accountant's office, and within six weeks the website was up and running. Building relationships with banks was relatively easy, because they viewed us as a potential supplier of customers for their lending products. What was much harder was coming up with ways to determine what banks and which of their products made the most sense for our clients.

I know that the difference between a good loan and a bad loan can be life or death for a business owner. In many ways, my team and I are business "doctors." We have put in time and gained a lot of experience so we can help our clients stay healthy and successful. We want our clients to have conversations with us so we can thoroughly understand their business and help them with the financing options available.

Our goal has been to help make business lending more clear and transparent. Our job is to know about all of the loan products available and help business owners put together debt structures that will accomplish their objectives. Like doctors, the professionals at MultiFunding gather information from our clients, discuss diagnoses and options, and then work collaboratively to steer them to the financing solutions we think will serve them best.

Since our founding, we've helped business owners get more than seven hundred loans, totaling around $300 million. It's satisfying to help business owners keep their dreams alive and their employees fed, and to operate with the best possible debt structures.

THE GROWTH DILEMMA

If you ask me to describe the primary tension that has kept me awake over the past eight years as I have built my company, it is whether I am investing fast enough to ensure the best long-term viability of my business.

Some entrepreneurs, like the first FishPreneur we met earlier, don't stay awake worrying about this. They're in a rhythm—they're content with their life and happy with their lot. But most entrepreneurs aren't like that. They always want something more for their business, though they're not sure what to do, how quickly to do it, how much risk to take, and how to fund it.

As in most tough decisions or issues that we struggle with, our real issue is not readily apparent, and we often hide behind an excuse. The most common story I hear is, "I would like to do this and that for my business, but I don't have the money to do it." But the money is often not the problem at all, or it is the easiest thing to solve.

TURN THE QUESTION ON ITS HEAD

Sometimes the best way to push through a challenging issue is to turn a question on its head. The way I do this is to ask entrepreneurs: "If I gave you $1 million, how would you invest it and what return would you expect from it?"

A corollary we will also ask is: "If your company could borrow $1 million at 6 percent interest, would you do it? Where would you invest it?"

This is the core question you will find as a common thread throughout this book. Its intent is to push you out of your comfort zone and challenge your assumptions about how you think about investing in your business and what your priorities are.

As you go through each section of this book, I encourage you to take a few minutes and answer the questions for yourself. At the same time, read the stories of the other entrepreneurs who have shared their answers and perspectives with us. Their insights might also help you to challenge your own thinking—perhaps even to come to a new conclusion.

OTHER QUESTIONS FOR YOU TO ANSWER

While the million-dollar question is a critical component of helping you think through the Rubik's Cube of your personal growth dilemma, other dimensions need to be considered: how long you plan to stay in business, what lifecycle stage your business is in, how comfortable you are with risk, and how fast you want to grow. Each section will pose questions so you can identify which type of entrepreneur you are.

ARE YOU A TORTOISE OR A HARE?

Do you consider yourself to be a tortoise or a hare entrepreneur? Hare entrepreneurs are focused on quick exits, cashing out, and moving on. In that case, equity may be a sound idea.

Tortoise entrepreneurs want to make long-term investments (financial and emotional) into what they're creating. They're likely to be the type who prefers taking on debt and pursuing the slow-growth approach.

YOUR LIFECYCLE STAGE

This section will help you think through your stage in the entre-preneurial lifecycle. Are you a glider, grower, speed-bumper, or exiter? Where you are personally will impact what your priorities are, which in turn will affect the way you think about investing in your business today.

YOUR RISK TOLERANCE

While it's fine and dandy for me to offer you a hypothetical gift of $1 million, the reality is that if you decide to invest in your busi-ness to generate faster growth, and you do that by raising some kind of equity or debt, it's going to come with risk. And often the issue that is masked in the growth dilemma is a legitimate and genuine fear of risk.

Take the time to get your risk score and decide how it's impact-ing your growth dilemma.

HOW MUCH GROWTH AND HOW FAST?

The final exercise is to measure your Growth Aspirations. Entrepreneurs think about growth in a variety of ways. Some are happy with modest growth, and others push hard for rocket-ship growth. There isn't a right answer, but the way you think about this influences your growth dilemma.

My hope for you is that you will take all of these elements and exercises and challenge yourself to find your financing comfort zone. Should you raise more money to grow your business faster? It's a complex and multidimensional issue that every entrepreneur needs to wrestle and struggle with. That's why it's helpful to read the stories of real entrepreneurs who, like you, have used these tools to help them find their financing comfort zones.

In the concluding section of the book, I will give you some tools and tips to think about, should you decide that borrowing or raising more money is the best choice for you.

A PERSONALIZED ASSESSMENT

As an additional resource, www.growthdilemma.com offers you a customized Growth Dilemma report. Once you're on the site, click the button on the top right corner of the home page to start your personalized assessment.

CHAPTER 1

The Million-Dollar Question

The first step in finding your financing comfort zone is to stop what you are doing and answer a challenging question.

Are you investing enough in your business? Does your business have enough capital to keep moving forward? Sometimes we need a tough question to shake up our thinking and challenge our routines.

Imagine that I presented you with a gift of $1 million. The one rule about the gift is that you cannot use it to buy a new house or a fancy car. You must invest it in your business or the mutual fund of your choice.

How would you divide the money, and what return would you expect from each investment?

HOW WOULD YOU INVEST YOUR NEXT $1 MILLION?

Step 1—How much $ will I invest in:

$	My Business
$	Mutual Fund

Step 2—Expected return from investment:

%	My Business
%	Mutual Fund

How you answer the question says a lot about how you feel about your business and whether you would try to expand if you had access to additional capital. Your response also speaks to what stage of life you are in, and whether you feel you can—and whether it's important to—diversify some of your risks and invest in things outside your business.

What return would you expect from your investment in the business and mutual fund? And what would you do with the money you put into your company? You might use it for additional sales staff, product development, acquisition, equipment, advertising, and so on.

If you expect a handsome return on your business investment and you have the option to raise equity or debt to make it happen, why aren't you doing it?

Asking yourself the million-dollar question is important for several reasons. If you're currently building and running a business, there are three things you can do with your next available dollar: You can spend it on something fun, you can reinvest it in your business, or—when you can afford to—you can take some chips off the table and diversify your risk. Often, we do not make these decisions thoughtfully and methodically.

You may be thinking about reinvesting in your business only through cash flow. If the returns are substantial and you are bullish on the prospects, adding debt (or perhaps equity) to your balance sheet may well be worth it.

ARE THESE DECISIONS EMOTIONAL OR RATIONAL?

While it's easy to create spreadsheets and models to make these decisions, the reality is that emotional components also enter into our thinking about money and risk.

Let me share an example.

Years ago, I had a client who ran a commercial cleaning company. We offered him a ten-year Small Business Administration (SBA) loan at a 6 percent interest rate that required a lien on his house. The other option was a one-year term loan at 36 percent without a lien on his house. He chose the latter. He had a past personal experience that led him to decide that, come hell or high water, he wasn't going to put a lien on his house.

Unfortunately, the short-term debt he chose caught up with him, and years later his business was in serious trouble. My client let the memory of a past event completely cloud the present in a way that ultimately harmed his business. Think about your prior experiences and how they influence the way you currently think about money and risk.

I know that having to watch the company where I'd worked for a decade completely blow up, with a thousand people losing their jobs, impacted how I think about risk and leverage. I am much happier letting my company grow slowly and organically, although I certainly risked everything to get it off the ground.

How do your past experiences impact the way you think about your million-dollar decision?

PROFILE: 'COREPHP'

As you can imagine, entrepreneurs answer the million-dollar question in many different ways—often with more emotion than a rational method. Michael Pignataro has, in my opinion, the most methodical answer to the million-dollar question of any entrepreneur profiled in this book.

As someone who once worked as a professional illusionist, Michael Pignataro knows how quickly money—among other things—can disappear. But that's not why, if he were given $1 million he could divide in any proportion between 'corePHP,' which he co-owns with his identical twin, Steven, and a mutual fund, he would only put 80 percent in 'corePHP.'

In 2001, Michael's twin founded the software development company 'corePHP,' which was originally based in Battle Creek, Michigan, and now also has an office in São Paulo, Brazil. As its name suggests, its initial focus was the PHP programming language, which it originally used to create custom content-management systems. Prior to 'corePHP,' Steven Pignataro had helped develop two open-source content-management systems: Mambo and one of its successors, Joomla!, which 'corePHP' still uses in web development.

Before they became business partners, Steven and Michael were performing as illusionists doing large-scale magic shows—until demand for the shows dropped off dramatically before the 2008 economic crash, causing them to cancel a tour while in the middle of it.

After getting off the road, Steven made 'corePHP' a limited liability company (LLC) with a business partner, and Michael went to work for a credit union. But when Steven wanted to ramp up the growth of 'corePHP' and his partner didn't, Michael borrowed money and bought out the partner.

Since then, 'corePHP' has developed an e-commerce platform for businesses called paGO Commerce. The company offers the platform for free, but users pay a small percentage on all customer transactions they conduct on it. Additionally, 'corePHP' offers development and marketing services to their paGo business clients and other businesses.

Michael said that after a few years of putting all his potential investment money into 'corePHP,' he wants to get back to the rule he's followed over the years, putting 80 percent of his available money into the business and 20 percent into other investments.

Although he would use the mutual fund for security, Michael would expect his investment in 'corePHP' to generate a return about 10 percent higher than the return generated by the mutual fund. The reason, he said, is that he expects that he'd be more focused on growing 'corePHP' than the managers of the mutual fund would be on growing the fund.

Michael said 'corePHP' is in the process of forming a joint venture to take paGO from being just an e-commerce platform to being a sales and marketing tool that will help its users increase their revenue. He expected 'corePHP' to have 2016 revenue of $1.2 million if it landed a couple of jobs that were pending when

I interviewed him, and $1 million to $1.1 million if it didn't. He also expected the company to be profitable.

His plans for the hypothetical $800,000 he'd invest in 'corePHP'? His first priority would be boosting its marketing and sales efforts. His second priority would be to continue developing and enhancing paGO so that it not only exceeds the demands of current 'corePHP' customers but ultimately reshapes the market for e-commerce platforms. The money would give 'corePHP' "the ability to scale faster than we're scaling right now."

On the other hand, when asked if he'd want to borrow $1 million at 6 percent interest, Michael said he probably wouldn't want the entire amount. His reason? He'd want to make sure the company could start paying back the loan right away, which it might not be able to do because of the revenue lag involved with paGO.

'corePHP' doesn't get money when businesses sign up to use the platform; it only profits when those businesses' customers start buying on the platform. Thus, it could run a marketing campaign that succeeded in bringing a lot of companies onto paGO without seeing much revenue from the effort for a few months. "When you're dealing with e-commerce, there's a ramp-up when users come on board."

REFLECTION

Unlike most entrepreneurs I've met and worked with, Michael has a methodical formula for deciding how much money to keep in and take out.

Do you have such a formula? If you don't, it's something to seriously consider.

CHAPTER 2

100 Percenters vs. Safety Netters

The entrepreneurs profiled in this book fit into one of two categories—100 percenters and safety netters.

The 100 percenters are those entrepreneurs who, when offered $1 million (whether as a gift or at a 6 percent interest rate) said they would, without hesitation, plunk it all down on their business.

The safety netters, on the other hand, were a bit more cautious. While they said they would invest most of the $1 million into their businesses, they all pledged to hold back varying amounts as a reserve.

But which approach is the right one?

Ultimately, you can make an argument that either approach is correct. It all depends upon intestinal fortitude, confidence, and personal preference.

It makes sense that many entrepreneurs fall into the 100 percenters category. To be an entrepreneur, you have to dream big, be willing to take risks, and have a high degree of confidence both in yourself and your business.

Here's a golf analogy that can shed light on this. Say you're on the green, about fifteen feet from the hole.

A cautious golfer might tap the ball too lightly which, in turn, means it cannot reach the cup.

A bold golfer will hit the ball harder. It may not go in—and it may go past the hole—but at least there's a chance it *will* go in.

In other words, if you aren't willing to take a risk (that the ball goes past the cup), there's no chance you can succeed (sink the putt).

Put many entrepreneurs on the golf course, and it's safe to say their putts aren't coming up short.

The confidence that 100 percenters express is appealing to some lenders, who want potential clients to believe in their businesses. That's the kind of mindset lenders can get behind.

Now let's look at the safety netters.

Obviously, there are some sound reasons for being at least somewhat cautious. An entrepreneur who would only invest $800,000 of the $1 million from our example, leaving a $200,000 cushion, is far from gun-shy.

An entrepreneur might have all the confidence in the world in their business, but they can never have 100 percent control, and unforeseen things can happen.

Can anyone predict that your warehouse and your entire inventory is going to burn when an electrical panel shorts out?

Can anyone know that the genius CEO who is building your company is going to drop dead from a heart attack even though he runs marathons, is a vegetarian, and has 7 percent body fat?

Can anyone be sure that demand for their luxury product won't crater when the economy unexpectedly tanks?

You get the idea.

It's never a bad idea to have a rainy-day fund. And while lenders look for entrepreneurs who have confidence in their business, many also prefer more measured types who might sacrifice a little growth for added security. After all, lenders are weighing risks and rewards too.

The bottom line is that there is no right answer: You have to trust your gut, weigh the specific circumstances of your business, and do what's best for you at that particular time and place.

Whatever you choose to do, however, accept the pros and cons and move forward confidently.

The following two profiles come from opposite ends of the spectrum—an all-in 100 percenter and an unapologetic zero percenter. Consider how their backgrounds influence their answers.

PROFILE: ASSOCIATION HEADQUARTERS

Since 2004, fifty-one-year-old Michael Dwyer has worked at Association Headquarters, a Mount Laurel, New Jersey, company that provides management and other services to trade associations and professional societies. He's currently the company's chief executive relationship officer and, along with its president and CEO, Bob Waller, the owner of 51 percent of it.

Association Headquarters runs the operations of thirty clients and has a significant number for which it provides a wide range of project-specific services, including marketing plans; meeting planning; and human resources, finance, and accounting work. Its full-service business still provides most of its revenue, but its project work is its fastest-growing segment.

Dwyer and Waller, who joined the company in 1987, just completed the process of buying out Bill MacMillan, the chairman of Association Headquarters, which he founded in 1978.

It's not surprising, therefore, that if Dwyer were given $1 million that he could split between Association Headquarters and a mutual fund of his choice, he would put all the money in Association Headquarters. "We have designs to grow, to continue to grow organically, but also to grow via acquisition, and so it could conceivably be used as part of an acquisition strategy. A lot of my future earnings potential is tied up in the success of the company, and I'd want to invest in that."

Association Headquarters provides a wide menu of services to trade associations and similar groups that represent various industries and professions. Its customers typically aren't big enough to have many, if any, full-time staffers, and their officers are volunteers who usually have full-time jobs as executives at companies in the industries the associations represent.

In 2011, Dwyer and Waller started buying out MacMillan, and they concluded the process in 2017.

The company employs nearly two hundred people, and it was set to turn a profit on revenue of $21 million in 2016, according to Dwyer. "Our profitability is somewhat limited by the business model that we have, but nonetheless, we've figured out a formula to keep our clients happy and still make a profit."

Dwyer said he feels he has a good ten years left to continue to invest in and grow with the company, and then after that, he feels he could still be valuable to Association Headquarters, whether he owns a piece of it or not.

He said he has no timetable for exiting his investment in Association Headquarters, which is not surprising, as he's still increasing it. But if the company is growing the way he thinks it can in ten years and is as profitable as he thinks he and Waller can make it, he wouldn't refuse an offer for his stake. "I think the future holds multiple possibilities."

If Dwyer had the opportunity to borrow up to $1 million at 6 percent for Association Headquarters, he'd take the full amount.

"We're in the midst of borrowing around $7 million now at around 4 percent, so what's another million?" Dwyer said he'd either use the funds to pay off existing debt or seek an acquisition opportunity to put them to use.

A CONTRASTING PROFILE: ARTISTS FRAME SERVICE

At the age of sixty-one, with four separate companies and 110 employees under his purview, Jay Goltz can be classified as happy to stay out of the fast lane. He is also a blogger for *Forbes*, a speaker, and the author of *The Street-Smart Entrepreneur: 133 Tough Lessons I Learned the Hard Way.*

"My goal is to get out of debt and be ready for the next recession," he said, indicating that his credit line is clear except for one building mortgage. "I'm looking to play it safer. I'm becoming conservative."

That's why Goltz said that if he were offered the hypothetical $1 million as a gift, it would all go into a mutual fund. And if given the opportunity to borrow up to $1 million at 6 percent to put into his business, he'd pass entirely.

"Cash is valuable, and my business is growing fast enough," he said, noting that a mutual fund could be expected to provide a long-term return of 7 percent. And if he needed cash, he could borrow against it while interest rates remain low. "I would be hesitant to borrow money on something that wouldn't provide a good return," he added.

Goltz has been an entrepreneur since graduating from college in 1978 when he opened Artists Frame Service, a company offering custom framing. Within a decade, he was generating $2 million annually in sales. Over the years, he's built out his profitable empire to more than $15 million in sales, buying four buildings and adding Chicago Art Source (corporate and gallery services), Jayson Home (modern and vintage furniture and home goods), and Bella + Prisma (wholesale moulding and frames) to his impressive stable of offerings.

While Goltz shies away from debt now, he said he's used it along the way to grow. "I was a junkie; I liked borrowing," he said.

But he's also had some bad experiences with debt and cautions entrepreneurs to be careful. At one point, his bank of eight years, which he was counting on to lend him several hundred thousand dollars in order to buy a warehouse, pulled out the day before closing. A friend agreed to lend Goltz $300,000, bailing him out of the situation. "Anyone who thinks the bank is your friend is naïve," he said, adding that banks don't necessarily need to care about your business plan; they're usually only truly interested in your equity and cash flow. One way to be able to tell you're at the wrong bank is to see if your representative changes every year, there's no workout department, and/or the bank makes few loans. Goltz recommends looking for banks that provide SBA-backed loans, as many banks just don't specialize in small-business loans.

"Math will be your friend, or math will be your enemy. There's a smart way of borrowing money, and there's a naïve way of borrowing money," Goltz shared. "That means it's imperative to find someone to explain the ins and outs of borrowing, including SBA loans, term loans, credit lines, mortgages, and leasing."

"But if you're going to have a hard time getting a loan, you probably should think twice before you pursue that," he said.

Over time, Goltz has observed that many successful businesses never borrow. He notes that slow and steady growth can often be better for a company than faster growth, especially if you keep control and understand that venture capital and partners can lead to unexpected problems and lack of control. Although borrowing can sometimes be appropriate in the right situation, he advises overall that you should take pains to be careful.

"The ignorance of debt causes tremendous, unnecessary grief, and it's frustrating to watch. Using debt is a great thing. It's a balancing act; it's a science and an art," he said.

REFLECTION

Dwyer at Association Headquarters would take the entire $1 million and use it to focus on acquisitions. This can be a good growth strategy, and a company's ability to borrow can be based on the cash flow of the existing business and the target.

Do you have an acquisition strategy or plan for your business?

On the other end of the spectrum, Goltz at Artists Frame Service wants none of that hypothetical $1 million. In fact, he's the only one featured in this book who answered our question this way. Why? He has been around the block—more than a few times.

Does Goltz's opinion make you reconsider your answer? Take a minute and give it some thought.

YOUR TURN: WHAT WOULD YOU DO?

How would you answer the million-dollar question? Whether a gift, a loan, or your own profits, what would you choose: to invest in your company or to invest in a mutual fund of your choice? What returns on investment would you expect from each?

Are you a 100 percenter or a safety netter? Are you bold, willing to take a chance on sinking all your money into your business? Or are you more cautious, preferring a wait-and-see attitude? As a golfer approaching a putt, do you tend to overshoot (bold) or undershoot (cautious)?

If your current way of thinking isn't serving you, how might you change that?

Here's one more profile for the chapter, this time from someone who falls in between the previous 100 percenter and the zero percent safety netter.

Sometimes entrepreneurs can't answer the million-dollar question, because while they'd like to put the money into their business, they're not sure what they would do with it. That's the situation with David Cooperberg.

PROFILE: IMACUCLEAN

I n 2003, business consultant David Cooperberg took on a new client, a residential-cleaning company called Imacuclean, which was based in Manhattan, where he lives.

Two months into the job, he asked Imacuclean's owner and founder, Gladys Berkley, what she wanted to do with it. She told him she wanted to sell it so she could concentrate on her interior-design firm. (She was eighty-two at the time.) The company was so small that Cooperberg didn't think anyone would want to buy it.

Then an idea occurred to him. "I thought, 'Maybe I should buy it.' I had been working out of my home, and I thought, 'I'll buy the company. It will take maybe 40 percent of my time, and I'll have an office,'" he said.

Cooperberg bought Imacuclean for what he said was a modest price in 2004. Despite his intentions, it quickly became his full-time occupation—he's now its president—and a good one. He said the company's sales had grown to eight figures by 2016, and it was profitable.

Still, if Cooperberg were given $1 million and told he could divide it in any proportion between Imacuclean and alternative investments that pay 3 to 4 percent (he doesn't invest in mutual funds), he said he'd probably put it all in the investments until he found a specific use for it at Imacuclean—even though he thinks putting the money in the company would generate a return of 20 to 30 percent.

"I would look at it and say, 'Gee, I found some segregated money. Let's concentrate on looking at opportunities in the business and thinking of how this money could be deployed into the business.' By the same token, my perspective is exit strategies from the business, so for me to put more money in the business is somewhat counterproductive," he said.

When Cooperberg bought out Imacuclean's original owner, the company primarily cleaned residences. Today, residential cleaning represents only 1 percent of its business. Most of its revenue now comes from providing cleaning staff to hotels, especially ones with spas and bars. "If you check into one of our client hotels, you won't even know we're there, because our workers are wearing the hotel uniforms."

Cooperberg said he would consider opportunities to take Imacuclean into other geographic areas, but with two caveats:

1. Imacuclean would have to land contracts to service enough rooms in one or more hotels in a region in order to justify the additional overhead required to set up shop there.

2. He would give preference to areas that are closer to New York (like South Jersey, for instance).

"If three hotels in southern Nevada said, 'We've heard great things about you guys and want you to come out and staff them for us,' we could achieve that because we could do it without having to burden ourselves with overhead," he said.

Not surprisingly, if Cooperberg were able to borrow up to $1 million at 6 percent for Imacuclean, he wouldn't borrow any of the money. "It's higher than our current borrowing cost," he said. "If we needed money for anything, we would just draw down the line of credit. If I needed money for five years, 6 percent would probably look good, but at the present time I don't."

REFLECTION

Sometimes entrepreneurs would like to put the money into their business but don't know what to do with it. It's a fair and legitimate answer, and you should never take on a term loan without a plan for how to pay it back and profit from it.

If you were to receive an infusion of cash, what would your plan be?

CHAPTER 3

What Does Money Have to Do with It?

Are you an entrepreneur who desires growth but feels stuck where you are? Do you know what is holding you back?

Often, when it comes to growing a company, the trigger is a fear of investment, taking on debt, or ruining the status quo. If you know what you need to do to grow your business, have a strong case for expecting a good return on your investment, can borrow the money to do it, and believe the expected return is higher than the cost of capital, then what is holding you back?

How much money are you investing in the future growth of your business today? Are you making enough investments today to ensure the long-term viability and growth of your business? This is the growth dilemma. It's a tough question without easy answers—and the goal of this book is to help guide you through it.

Is money a crutch?

In the early stages of many businesses, I often find that entrepreneurs get stuck thinking they need a lot more money to get going than they actually do. Instead of struggling to raise or borrow $1 million to accomplish A, B, and C, they might be much better off just pulling together enough money to do A, which will start to prove their concept and get some cash flowing.

In some ways, raising money or borrowing money can be a crutch: Everyone seems to think that more money will solve all things. And sometimes the process of hunting for the money, or looking for the wrong amount of money, becomes the focus and dominates everything.

I spoke to a woman once who had invented a horse shampoo and was at the point of wanting to produce it and sell it. She had spent the only $40,000 she had to write a business plan to help her raise $5 million. She wanted to buy a building, buy the equipment, hire a management team, and start production.

The problem: She didn't have a customer.

Whoever took that $40,000 for her business plan should be banned from ever helping an entrepreneur again. This woman needed a customer, a purchase order, and a co-packing facility before she could get started.

She needed to prove her concept before anyone would give her the kind of money she needed to begin. But by raising the money instead of building her business, she lost her shirt *and* her dream.

THE FINANCING TIPPING POINT

At some point, after the first few years of struggling, the converse happens. You could benefit from more money than you think you need in order to keep your business pushing forward.

At later stages in the company's lifecycle, when you have started to prove ideas and concepts, there can be a real need for and benefit to expansion capital. As an entrepreneur, you either have the no-debt badge of honor (meaning you have never taken on debt or have completely paid off any debt you did take on) or you're used to your routine and can't think outside your box to find ways to expand and grow.

The opposite story to the horse shampoo woman is an entrepreneur who owns and runs an engineering consulting firm. He could double his business if he chose to double his team. But he doesn't think he has the capital to do it. However, he has $5 million of accounts receivable at any time and operates his business on a $100,000 line of credit. He could walk into any bank in town and get a $4 million line of credit. But he is afraid of the risk.

This book will help you understand whether you are putting the appropriate amount of capital to work to help get your business to the next level. There are tough choices you must consider, such as how much leverage and risk you need and feel comfortable with, as you consider your own growth dilemma.

The following profile proves the point that money isn't the solution to everything. Nate Kukla has an interesting perspective on the core question. He would take the $1 million, but not without hiring the right person to oversee its implementation. He is right that access to capital is not the only answer to push growth. It's just one ingredient in the mix.

PROFILE: UNIQUE INDOOR COMFORT

As the president of a residential heating and air-conditioning company, Nate Kukla spends a lot of time concerning himself with other people's comfort. When it comes to taking on risk, his comfort level is quite high.

Kukla, who co-owns Unique Indoor Comfort with his uncle, Frank Mutz, said that if he were offered $1 million that he could divide between his business and a mutual fund, he would put all the money into his business. "We're young and growing, so it would give a very good return on investment."

Kukla began working with his uncle eleven years ago. He was employed by Johnson & Johnson and living in Norfolk, Virginia, but small business intrigued him, so when he learned at a family gathering that the partners in his uncle's company, Unique Indoor Comfort, were looking for a sales manager, he applied for and got the job.

After five years, Kukla and his uncle left the company they were with and started a new Unique Indoor Comfort based in Conshohocken, a former mill town about five miles northwest of Philadelphia. Since then, Kukla has grown Unique Indoor Comfort to $8.6 million in annual revenue and forty-seven employees. His uncle has an advisory role with the company and remains a partner in it.

Although Kukla would put all of the hypothetical $1 million into Unique Indoor Comfort and none into the mutual fund, he said he didn't know the return he'd expect from either. "I could certainly double the business in a couple of years, but it's easier said than done. Having the money doesn't guarantee anything; it's finding the right person to head up that development," he asserts.

Kukla would first use the money to buy a headquarters for Unique Indoor Comfort. After that, he'd bring on someone to head up a training program that would teach technical and soft skills so his company could add qualified staffers. "People are key to this industry, and it's not always easy to find solid, experienced people. The best thing to do is find good people, develop them, and give them the necessary skills," he said.

"The shortage of qualified workers is a bottleneck to growth for many companies in the heating and cooling industry," Kukla said. Even if Unique Indoor Comfort were to land enough jobs to enable it to double its revenue, it wouldn't be able to take them all on because it doesn't have enough technicians. "If we could have unlimited resources and an unlimited bench of quality individuals, then we really could double in a couple of years."

In addition to enabling expansion of its Philadelphia-area operations, Kukla thinks being able to find good people and provide them with quality training would allow Unique Indoor Comfort to open branches in other areas. If the company already had the platforms and systems to support its staff, the company could take on counterparts in other areas that want to join it—or even branch out into other industries.

As a result of his belief in his company's possibilities, Kukla said that if he could borrow up to $1 million at 6 percent annual interest to invest in Unique Indoor Comfort, he would borrow the entire amount.

REFLECTION

Many entrepreneurs are stuck where they are because they don't know how to approach the discussion about funding their business. Would more money help? Or are they putting the chicken before the egg? Do they really need something more basic—a sound product, a customer base, a business plan?

Are you ready to consider tough questions as you consider your own growth dilemma?

CHAPTER 4

Are You a Tortoise or a Hare?

Do you remember "The Tortoise and the Hare," one of Aesop's fables? In this tale, an arrogant hare ridicules a slow-moving tortoise. The tortoise challenges the hare to a race, which the hare readily accepts. When the race begins, the hare jumps out to a huge lead, but overconfidently decides to stop to rest and inadvertently falls asleep. He awakens to find the steadily moving tortoise has won the race.

What does this have to do with business? Plenty, it turns out.

It seems when it comes to entrepreneurs, there are two kinds—hares and tortoises.

Which kind are you?

TORTOISE ENTREPRENEURS

 As you might guess, tortoise entrepreneurs are more likely to be cautious and less likely to take risks. Their goal is to pursue gradual growth over a spread-out time span.

My role models have always been tortoise entrepreneurs. They don't think about their business in the short term. For them, it's a long-term venture and a legacy, requiring patience and persistence. They are not thinking about the next quarter or round of financing; they will do what it takes to strengthen their company for the long run. Their business is their baby. And they won't give it up easily.

Debt financing tends to be the preferred form of funding for this kind of entrepreneur. Typically, investors are more excited about backing hares than they are tortoises, so often the only choice for a tortoise is to borrow money.

That's not necessarily a bad thing—debt financing is less risky than granting equity positions to investors, which means selling a piece of the business and thus losing some control over it.

Entrepreneurs who want to use debt need to keep a few things in mind.

First off, keep your business books in pristine order. No lender wants to work with any business owners with suspect bookkeeping.

Pay attention to your credit, especially in the start-up phase. Your personal history will carry more weight with lenders because your personal finances will be considered a longer-term snapshot of your ability to manage money.

Meanwhile, create a path to bankability—the things a lender

is most likely to peruse. This includes business profitability, credit history, collateral, and cash flow. The more details you can provide, the better.

A few more points to consider as you look into raising cash:

- Open a home-equity line of credit to tap into cheap and easy money.

- Review your debt regularly. What makes sense right now might not in six months. Always look to structure loans for maximum flexibility.

- Ask yourself if you need the money. Loans aren't always the solution to every problem.

PROFILE OF A TORTOISE: TYGA-BOX SYSTEMS

Your company has developed a product that has the potential to help its industry solve one of its customers' most persistent and frustrating problems. You're offered $1 million that you can divide in any proportion between your company and a mutual fund. Where would you put the money?

Many entrepreneurs would go for it all and put the entire $1 million in their company. Not Nadine Cino. She'd put $200,000 in the mutual fund as a safety net.

That's not surprising coming from someone who has co-owned her business for a quarter century. Cino and her partner, Marty Spindel, founded Tyga-Box Systems in 1991 and still have an 85 percent stake in the New York-based company. She, therefore, is approaching an age when many entrepreneurs start formulating exit plans.

Not only do Cino and Spindel *not* have exit plans, they believe Tyga-Box Systems is poised to launch a radio frequency identification (RFID) technology that has the potential to be adopted by the moving and storage industry the world over. It would make item tracking part of everyday life.

The technology is designed to enable users to easily follow every item they move so they don't lose track of anything, regardless of whether it's in transit or in storage. It doesn't require permanent infrastructure, force users to change their way of doing things, or require in-depth training sessions. Instead, it simply uses the clients' mobile phones to track the locations of the items they're moving and/or storing.

The technology isn't the first invention of Cino's that targets the moving industry. That honor goes to the Tyga-Box System that she and Spindel, president and cofounder of Tyga-Box Systems, came up with after a discussion about the moving industry while they were going through a move themselves.

The system consists of hard plastic TygaBoxes, which are reusable, and TygaDollies, which are designed to hold nothing but TygaBoxes. Users put a box onto a dolly, load and close it, put another box on top of it, and repeat the process. This means they never have to lift a box unless it's empty. The boxes can be stacked five high so they use vertical space in trucks more efficiently than corrugated cardboard boxes, which Cino said can be stacked only three high, or the plastic boxes in moving systems used by Tyga-Box's competitors, which she said can be stacked only four high.

When Cino and Spindel came up with the idea for Tyga-Box Systems, she was expanding her international fashion-design consultancy, and he was in his seventeenth year at a Manhattan law firm where he specialized in trusts, estates, and philanthropic grant making. They have since built the company into a going concern that Cino said is profitable and generates from $1.3 to $1.8 million in revenue per year.

Cino thinks TygaTrax will enable Tyga-Box Systems to grow dramatically. The reason, she said, is because TygaTrax does something that hasn't been done in the RFID world: It combines two kinds of tracking on a single platform. One kind of tracking is long range, enabling users to identify all the pieces of equipment on a floor, for example. The other is more location specific, allowing users to identify the room or cubicle a piece of equipment is in.

In addition to appealing to moving and storage companies, she believes TygaTrax will appeal to property managers and managers of facilities such as hospitals, which have lots of expensive equipment for which the location must be known at all times.

Tyga-Box Systems tested TygaTrax in its own warehouse and on local moves. And in December 2016, the company showcased the system on a move that Bank of America Merrill Lynch made in Cincinnati. "The TygaTrax showcase with Bank of America Merrill Lynch has been a 100 percent success. We tracked 2,260 TygaTrax boxes over three weeks, five locations, seven floors, 150,000 square feet, and multiple truckloads on a twenty-four-seven basis, and every single item was returned to close out the project without missing anything," said Cino.

Coincidentally, Tyga-Box Systems financed the development of the software for TygaTrax with an SBA loan from Bank of America Merrill Lynch. Cino said the software was 92 percent done, but its user interface needed to be improved.

The company financed the development of the TygaTrax hardware with its own money. In addition to custom-engineered tags, the hardware includes local wireless gateways about the size of nightlights that can be plugged into wall sockets so workers don't have to leave their phones in places overnight to monitor items. Cino said Tyga-Box Systems deployed $150,000 of equipment at the TygaTrax showcase in Cincinnati.

Tyga-Box Systems is looking to raise $1 million to help develop final versions of its tags so it can commercialize TygaTrax. The system could be ready for commercial deployment by March. The company also wants to use the money it raises to get versions of TygaTrax deployed in a few cities "to seed the market," Cino said.

Tyga-Box Systems has invitations to perform trials of TygaTrax with Amazon.com, Procter & Gamble, and other Fortune 100 companies. Anticipating that those trials will go well, Cino thinks the company can increase its valuation from $7.5 to $20 million and raise an additional $5 million. It also has some lease financing that will allow it to roll out ten thousand to thirty thousand Tyga-Trax tags to mover customers, if it chooses to do that.

Although Cino said that if she were given $1 million, she would put only $800,000 of it in Tyga-Box Systems, she said that if she could borrow up to $1 million at 6 percent to invest in the company, she would take the entire amount and use it for marketing TygaTrax. "We all know first-to-market advantage is only as good as your marketing," she said.

Her willingness to commit money at an age at which many entrepreneurs would be thinking about retirement makes her a tortoise.

REFLECTION

Living the life and adventure of a builder entrepreneur is similar to running a marathon. It's fascinating that twenty-six years into her journey, Cino would still take the majority of her $1 million and invest it in her business.

Do you think your age or how long you have been in your business impacts how you would think about your decision?

HARE ENTREPRENEURS

There's nothing wrong with thinking big—and hare entrepreneurs want to grow as big as possible as quickly as they can.

More often than not, that means equity financing—money that could come from venture capitalists, angel investors, private equity, or other sources.

The media often refer to this type of quick-rise company as a *unicorn*, and such businesses are often touted by the media. Unicorns often risk it all to build billion-dollar companies. They may jump on the venture-capital treadmill, which typically involves multiple rounds of financing. In these cases, years or even decades of losses are typical as the company focuses on growth and market share.

Hare entrepreneurs typically want to build several ventures in their careers—quickly—and then sell them. They're more passionate about the process than about the actual entity they're building. Their goal in life is multiple exits. The game is to get in and get out. They would never put up their house as collateral for their latest venture, because they're not that emotionally tied to their company.

Lining up that investment money means spending time to craft management teams and business plans that appeal to those investors. That wooing process will become part of your everyday business game plan because you'll be answering to those new masters who have agreed to bankroll you.

That process isn't for everyone, so hare entrepreneurs need to think carefully before choosing the equity path.

PROFILE OF A HARE: BENEFITRFP

When asked how much of a $1 million gift he'd put in his company and how much he'd put in a mutual fund, the CEO of benefitRFP, Bob Nienaber, didn't hesitate.

"If I can take a million and get a twenty-five-time multiple on it, you know where I'd put it," he said.

In other words, Nienaber would put it all in his company, a cloud-based service provider of executive benefit plan products and services. The money would go to further building out the company's platforms.

Similarly, if Nienaber could borrow up to $1 million at 6 percent interest, he'd borrow all of it.

"With interest costs so low, there's no sense in an equity play or dealing with a hedge fund," he said.

That said, Nienaber—on principle—doesn't spend a lot of time worrying about financing.

"If a company is strong enough, you don't need outside funding," he maintains. "Build on your own merits—survive or fail."

In fact, benefitRFP has done a lot more than just survive in a fast-changing industry. Nienaber had years of expertise in the field—he helped create the platforms and sales operations for Guardian, Principal Financial Group, and Phoenix Companies of America—when he founded the company with Chief Operating

Officer Steffen Nass in 2006. The two remain the only shareholders in benefitRFP, which was incorporated in 2009.

Though the company, based in Sacramento, California, remains small with only five employees, its reach is much larger.

"We have relationships with people who bring us preferred partner agreements," Nienaber said, indicating that benefitRFP has a dozen arrangements with companies that act as franchisees.

A typical client for benefitRFP is a privately held company with annual revenue anywhere from $50 million to perhaps $2 billion.

"A lot of privately held companies need programs to lock in top people and set up benefits," he said. "I've always tried to target that group."

The company relies on technology to maintain an edge, particularly a program called benefitMATRIX™. Nienaber said the program is used to educate clients on all facets of executive benefit plans while identifying the administrative and funding requirements that work best with each client. This technology employs proprietary algorithms to help determine the best match.

The year 2017 was full of changes for benefitRFP, which merged with BD Capital Partners LLC, a Cincinnati-based acquirer of independent insurance agencies.

"We had a lot of offers—maybe eighty offers," said Nienaber, who indicated a goal of his is to be part of a billion-dollar business.

The combined company's revenue is about $100 million, with benefitRFP collecting about $30 million in January premiums.

Nienaber is most definitely a fast-moving hare.

His goals are aggressive: The merged company will generate a little more than $100 million in insurance premium revenue, but he hopes to boost that to $1 billion per year within five years.

Nienaber believes that's achievable for many reasons, but the most important one is that his company has no real competitors. The fact that many human resources departments don't understand how benefits programs work doesn't hurt, either.

"We're the only cloud-based executive benefit company," he said, adding that their systems are trademarked.

Whatever the future holds, Nienaber expressed confidence he and his company, not to mention his new business partners at BD Capital, are up to the task—with or without outside funding.

"If we can build the technology to save the need for actuaries and so on, we'll prove our value," he said.

OVERALL

You might be able to tell that my preferred modus operandi is the tortoise entrepreneur.

While the media likes to focus on those companies that skyrocket out of nowhere, it isn't reporting on all the businesses that choose the fast-growth path only to crash and burn.

Far more businesses succeed by moving slowly and steadily. Remember that many companies take years to mature; rare is the company that develops immediately and shows a healthy bottom line.

A 2015 American Express OPEN Small Business Growth Pulse survey of entrepreneurs with at least $250,000 in annual sales found that growth was a priority for 72 percent. Still, 63 percent of respondents said they preferred the slow, steady approach, while just 25 percent planned to be aggressive.[1]

There's never only one path to success. Both the tortoise and hare approaches have positive and negative aspects, and your kind of business may dictate the path you take—tech companies typically follow the hare approach, for example. More conventional businesses often pursue the tortoise approach. Choose your path and be comfortable with it. If you've elected to be a tortoise, don't act like a hare and try funding approaches that won't fit for you. Or vice versa.

REFLECTION

A key distinction for any entrepreneur: Are you a tortoise or a hare? The tortoise is interested in gradual growth, is not afraid of debt financing, and keeps good records to show the business is well run and profitable.

Hare entrepreneurs, on the other hand, want to grow—fast. They often depend on equity financing from outside investors, which means they need appealing management teams and business plans.

It's often tempting to jump on the hare train because it sounds sexier and simpler. Hare success stories are often what we read about in the news. But it's important to pick your path and stick

---

1   American Express News, "Small Business Owners Say Growth Is Their Top Priority, Reports American Express OPEN Research," *American Express News: Press Release,* accessed September 16, 2015, http://about.americanexpress.com/news/pr/2015/small-business-growth-top-priority-open.aspx.

to it because what you choose will determine what financing tools you'll need.

So, are you a tortoise or a hare?

CHAPTER 5

Where Are You in Your Business Journey?

How you think about your growth dilemma is often tied to where you are in your entrepreneurial journey. After having the honor of working with thousands of entrepreneurs over the last several years, I generally find that they fall into four categories: growers, gliders, speed-bumpers, and exiters. How do you identify yourself?

Understanding where you are in the lifecycle is helpful, because it influences how you think about your growth dilemma and how to hone in on your financing comfort zone. As an example, if you're an exiter, you don't have a dilemma—you've already decided to get out. Likewise, if you're a glider, as described below, you're already in your financing comfort zone.

Let's take a closer look at these lifecycle stages.

GROWERS

The grower is the most common type of entrepreneur—or at least it is the most common type among entrepreneurs who take the time to go to conferences or take part in seminars related to their businesses. When asked what they'd do with their $1 million gift, they invariably say they'd put all or almost all of it in their business and not have a second thought. It's in their DNA.

Personally, I am a grower. I can't help myself. I am constantly thinking about new ideas and ways to grow and expand my business. It's both a blessing and a curse. The blessing is that it leads to a creative and stimulating life. The curse is that sometimes it's hard to focus on what's working because you're always thinking about the next idea. And being a grower doesn't typically lead to much work/life balance.

In fact, most of the entrepreneurs we've already profiled are growers: Michael Pignataro of 'corePHP,' Michael Dwyer of Association Headquarters, Nate Kukla of Unique Indoor Comfort, Nadine Cino of Tyga-Box Systems, and Bob Nienaber of benefitRFP.

GLIDERS

Glider entrepreneurs have businesses that are in pretty good shape. They're happy with their companies. They like the money their businesses are producing for them, and they don't want to mess around with that. A glider might put some or all of the $1 million in their business if they saw some opportunities to deploy it there or if they were fully confident that the company would provide them with a higher return on the money than they could get from a mutual fund. Then again, like the CEO of Imacuclean, David Cooperberg (profiled in chapter 2), they might park the money in investments until they see how their business could make use of it. In their minds, they're content with where they are.

I have a friend I consider to be in the glider category. He runs his business and works about thirty hours a week. Every summer he vacations in Europe for about a month and goes off the grid. He makes enough money to live on and save. It's not in my DNA to live the way he does, but I admire him for finding such balance.

SPEED-BUMPERS

Speed-bumper entrepreneurs have businesses that have hit a patch of rough road and need a cash infusion. They still believe in their companies—otherwise they wouldn't be willing to commit all or nearly all the $1 million to them—but their belief isn't the only thing driving their decision. American Fire Glass, profiled later in the book, is a good example of a speed-bumper's company. A confluence of events in the industry, along with bank fatigue, led to the bank calling its loan. But the owner of the company, Matt Doll, thinks the industry is growing. He is a leader in the industry, and he believes his company is in a position to turn a profit this year.

If you want to think about a speed-bumper, consider the taxi driver I met a few months ago late one night in the dead of winter in Omaha, Nebraska. When I landed at the airport, my iPhone battery was dead. I did the old-fashioned thing and jumped in a cab instead of ordering an Uber. That poor driver had been waiting for hours for a passenger while dozens of Ubers passed him by. Technology had speed-bumped him, but sadly he had not adjusted.

EXITERS

Exiter entrepreneurs are tired of running a business or think the company they lead has run its course, and they are looking to sell their stake in it. Jay Goltz, who started the first of his Chicago-area art-related businesses in 1978 and whom we described as a zero percent safety netter in chapter 2, is one of only two exiters profiled in this book.

PROFILE OF A GROWER: TELEX METALS

M att Danish got into the metals business serendipitously. He needed a job, and a family member introduced him to someone who was looking for people to set up and manage recycling accounts. That was in 2001. In 2010, he started Telex Metals, and he hasn't looked back.

Telex specializes in minor metals. Minor metals, according to the Minor Metals Trade Association (MMTA), aren't traded on formal exchanges. (However, two metals—cobalt and molybdenum—are now being traded on the London Metal Exchange.)

Minor metals are produced in smaller quantities than base metals, such as iron and lead, and are often used in specialized (frequently high-tech) applications. Some uses include light-bulb filaments, computer and mobile-phone components, and tools used to cut steel.

Telex, which is based in Croydon, northeast of Philadelphia, processes metals three ways: dry processing, such as cutting and shearing; hydrometallurgy, which entails using aqueous chemistry to extract metals from ores, concentrates, and recycled materials; and pyrometallurgy, which involves using high temperatures to extract, purify, or change the form of metals. The company serves the electronics, medical, super-alloy, and hard-metals industries, doing everything from supplying metals to recycling them and helping customers manage their inventories.

The metal recycling, manufacturing, and refining company now employs fifteen people and is profitable. And when asked what he'd do if he were given $1 million that he could divide in any proportion between his business and a mutual fund, Danish said he'd put it all into Telex. "If we had $1 million, I'm confident that we could realize 10-20 percent returns annually."

A mutual fund, he said, would produce a return of only 2 to 10 percent, "if you don't lose 5 or 10 percent, or more should the market drop." Danish said he could use the money for capital expenditures or expansion of Telex's staff. "We're looking at processing equipment, at hiring the right people. Either of those is a good investment," he said.

As for the impact the sum would have on Telex, Danish said it would boost the company's profits by giving it more money to earn a return on as well as provide it with additional financial stability.

Danish is Telex's majority owner, but three other employees also have stakes in the company: John Gurule, chief operating officer; Lara Welgs, planning manager; and Jim Maguire, general manager.

Given the opportunity to borrow up to $1 million at 6 percent to put into Telex, Danish said he'd borrow the whole amount. But while he's not averse to taking on debt for Telex—as he said, the company has much more debt than the hypothetical $1 million—Danish has his limits. "If somebody would offer me $10 million, I wouldn't do it. I couldn't put that money to work comfortably."

Still, since Danish would borrow $1 million at 6 percent if he could and would put it all in Telex if he were given $1 million, he qualifies as a full-fledged grower.

REFLECTION

While Danish would willingly borrow the entire hypothetical $1 million, he wouldn't borrow $10 million. He understands his limits at the current stage of his business. The $1 million we use in this book is a benchmark. Depending on the size of your business, the appropriate number to think about is really up to you.

What is the ideal amount of money you would like to have to bolster your balance sheet?

PROFILE OF A GLIDER: CLICKAWAY

W hat's the difference between a tire- and auto-repair shop and a store that sells and repairs cell phones and offers computer, network, and IT services, among other things? If you said "everything," you're way off base. The real answer is "not much."

So says Rick Sutherland, the president and CEO of ClickAway, a Northern California–based chain with more than forty locations. Sutherland should know. At the age of nineteen, he cofounded a tire- and auto-repair shop and grew it to twenty-five locations before he sold it in 1999. Sure, there are some differences, as the tire and auto industry has many more insurance concerns and is a lot dirtier. A computer store is a lot cleaner than a garage.

But at their heart, both types of businesses need to offer good products and services at fair prices to succeed. And the nuts and bolts—things such as hiring, accounting, procuring parts, renting buildings, and so on—are the same. "Almost everything I learned in the auto industry from a business point of view transferred over to this," he said.

That includes confidence in his company. When asked what he would do if he were given $1 million to invest either in his business or a mutual fund, Sutherland said he'd invest all of it in his business—making him part of the 100 percenter group we discussed in chapter 2. Said Sutherland: "I can make a fair amount of return on money I invest in the business." That money likely would go for acquisitions and inventory as well as some remodeling and upgrading of existing stores. "A million would be significant. It would give us another eight to ten stores and maybe ten to fifteen million in revenue," he said.

Sutherland sold his previous business at age forty-three but said he was pretty miserable being retired, so in 2001 he started Click-Away as a computer service and repair shop for consumers and small businesses. The business grew quickly, although not always as expected. "My initial thought was we were always going to go on site, but customers started to come here," he said, noting that the initial location quickly grew into five stores.

A few years later, however, with the advent of the smartphone, the business evolved again, and Sutherland made the connection between smartphones, the internet, and computers. That led him to purchase a fourteen-store chain of Verizon Wireless stores and to turn the company's main focus toward cell phones. "Seventy-five percent of the business is now selling phones on the Verizon Wireless network."

As of December 1, 2016, Sutherland had forty-six ClickAway stores with more than two hundred employees, as well as a logistics division that manages a fleet of ten thousand laptops for a computer-camp company. ClickAway is set to break the $40 million mark in annual revenue and has generated healthy profits.

"We're pretty unique. We just do a lot of things. We do a lot of things that are very techy and will sell a lot of phones. We're going to continue to be focused on phones and repair work," he said.

While Sutherland has been able to tap into his clients' needs to help grow his businesses, he's also had to line up assorted credit lines of different amounts over the past forty years. Still, when asked how much he'd borrow if he could borrow up to $1 million at 6 percent, Sutherland said he'd likely borrow nothing, since he can already borrow at the prime rate plus 0.75 percent. (At the time of this writing, the prime lending rate is 4.25 percent.)

As for the future, Sutherland has no set goals, as he's happy with the current status of ClickAway. That would classify him as a glider. But since he'd still put all of the hypothetical $1 million gift in his business, he's a grower by nature. In other words, he's somewhere between being a grower and a glider.

"My company gives people a pretty good opportunity to make a lot of money," he said, adding that the business does require near-constant attention on his part. "I wouldn't mind taking a couple weeks off every year."

REFLECTION

Sutherland's story is interesting because he is somewhere in the middle of being a glider and a grower. About a third of entrepreneurs give more than one answer when asked where they fit. And sometimes when you are torn, it's tougher to answer the million-dollar question clearly.

If you seem to fall between two stages in the entrepreneurial lifecycle, it might help to think through your primary identifier.

PROFILE OF A SPEED-BUMPER:
AMERICAN FIRE GLASS

M att Doll may not be your traditional executive laden with experience and an MBA from a prestigious university, but when it comes to being an entrepreneur, he displays all the hallmark traits.

The man who dropped out of high school at the end of his sophomore year because he couldn't learn in a traditional environment is willing to take a risk and bet on himself. Doll is at the stage in his journey where he is not thinking about diversification or taking chips off the table.

When asked what he would do if given the choice of investing $1 million in his business or a mutual fund, he said there is no choice. All of it would go toward American Fire Glass, the fireplace/fire-pit glass and burner-products business based in Lake Elsinore, California, he founded thirteen years ago at the tender age of twenty-four.

"I'm 100 percent confident in myself, and I'm 100 percent confident that I can make more than other people investing could," Doll said, noting that he expected to double that investment within five years. "It would allow me to do the things I would dream about doing."

Doll's philosophy clearly places him in the grower category that's most prevalent among the entrepreneurs we surveyed.

The founder, president, and CEO of American Fire Glass said about two-thirds of the $1 million gift would go for inventory, adding that cash flow is his biggest bottleneck in completing sales. The remaining third would be spent on infrastructure—new technical systems for accounting and warehouse management—as well as some top-level hires.

And if that same $1 million were offered at a 6 percent interest rate?

Doll would make the same decision. "I'm confident I can make a whole lot more than 6 percent," he said.

Doll hasn't lacked for confidence since the time he was working as a construction laborer installing windows. That's when he noticed a guy making fireplace glass by breaking champagne bottles inside a pillowcase.

"I can do it better," he said.

It turns out he could, using tempered glass to create his own product.

Doll said he figured that if he could earn $16,000 in sales each month, he could go out on his own. Working from his garage, it took less than six weeks to reach that goal. And by the end of his first full year in 2004, he had generated about $600,000 in sales.

To grow, however, capital was required—and his first lending experience was a good one. In 2005, all it took was his signature to secure a $150,000 SBA-backed loan. Doll decided to live off that loan and plow all his earnings back into American Fire Glass.

For the next decade, the company averaged annual growth of 34 percent. As the company grew and added products to its offerings, more capital was needed, but efforts in 2012 and 2013 to obtain a loan were fruitless.

That changed in late 2014. That's when a major bank provided a $500,000 line of credit, which was bumped up to $1 million a year later, with a pledge it would be converted into an SBA loan.

Still expressing his trademark confidence, Doll began making strategic and long-term decisions, including increasing inventory and hiring staff.

Unfortunately, sales hit a plateau in 2016, and the bank pulled the line of credit—which American Fire Glass had already spent. Because Doll couldn't repay the credit line, the bank filed a lawsuit, demanding its money by July 1, 2017.

Other lenders were wary.

Fortunately, Doll recently secured a ten-year SBA-backed loan for $1.1 million to pay back the bank and a separate $350,000 SBA-backed line of credit for American Fire Glass.

With his company's financial health restored, Doll is again able to concentrate on his business, which is on pace for 22 percent growth in 2017. He has about forty-five employees, and projected sales in 2017 will be around $10.3 million, making the year a profitable one.

American Fire Glass spent its first six years focusing on its namesake product, but Doll had a revelation. "We realized almost everyone who was buying our product was either installing it in a fireplace or a fire pit," he said.

By 2010, the company added a line of stainless-steel burners for the do-it-yourself market. And in 2016, the company acquired California Outdoor Concepts, a leading high-end fire-pit manufacturer. That deal added $500,000 to American Fire Glass's debt sheets but will bring in an expected $1 million in sales.

"My goal is to be the biggest manufacturer of fire pits in the United States," Doll said.

The California Outdoor Concepts name will go on high-end pits selling for between $1,800 and $6,000, while American Fire Glass is negotiating a licensing agreement for mass-retail fire pits.

Three to five years from now, Doll, currently thirty-seven years old, hopes to add patio furniture to the product mix. Challenges include increased competition, especially in the fire-pit business where about twenty companies tread. The business may also become more vulnerable, as federal Environmental Protection Agency regulations have led some cities to ban the use of natural gas and propane in certain applications.

While the financial scare didn't shake Doll's confidence, he said it made him a better entrepreneur.

No longer does he make snap decisions without consulting his team. "I had one toe over the edge of losing everything," he said. "That changed me as a person. I'm changing the way I operate the business."

REFLECTION

If managed properly, a speed-bump is exactly that, a bump in the road. And then you push forward like Doll is doing.

Has your business recently gone through a speed-bump like Doll's? What is your plan to move through it?

PROFILE OF AN EXITER: CHRISTINE TAYLOR

I magine the following: You started your business in 1990, so you're thinking of exiting it in five to ten years. The company just had a bad year, as did the entire industry it's part of.

On top of that, your firm and its competitors service brick-and-mortar retailers, many of which are engaged in life-and-death struggles with Amazon and its online counterparts.

You're offered $1 million that you can divide in any proportion between your business and a mutual fund. What would you do with the money?

The seemingly prudent thing to do would be to put most, if not all, of it in the mutual fund.

When initially interviewed for this book, that's not what Christine Taylor would have done, and it's not because she's not prudent. Instead, Taylor thinks her industry's downturn is due to events that aren't likely to recur, and talk of its demise is premature. As a result, she'd put the entire $1 million in her company, Christine Taylor Collection, in part due to its 31.5 percent profit margin in 2015.

"My normal profit margin on $1 million is way higher than any mutual fund is going to pay me," Taylor said.

Christine Taylor Collection specializes in visual merchandizing; it designs and produces everything from props used in displays for retailers to entire displays.

The field is not one Taylor thought she'd be in.

She was a figure skater and thought she'd do that for her career, but changed her mind while earning a bachelor of fine arts degree from Rosemont College, a small liberal arts college about ten miles northwest of Philadelphia. After graduating, she got a job for the Christmas season with Bamberger's, a department-store chain that was subsequently bought by Macy's.

"My first day on the job, I knew I had found the niche I was looking for," she said. "I absolutely loved it and wanted to do it the rest of my life."

By the late 1980s, Taylor was an executive with Macy's on a team charged with opening new stores. She'd get to a store and want to decorate it, but there was no vendor she could call to make the pieces she wanted. So, she'd design them herself, buy raw materials from the contractors working on the store, and make them with her fellow Macy's executives.

The materials weren't cheap, and the time Taylor and the other Macy's executives spent to make the pieces wasn't cheap either, so Taylor knew Macy's was paying a lot of money for the decorations she was making.

"That's when the proverbial light bulb went off," she said. "I said, 'There's a void; perhaps I could fill it.'"

Taylor formulated the plans for her company in 1989 and left Macy's the following year to start it. She initially financed it with a small insurance payment she received when her car was stolen, but quickly got a $10,000 bank loan, then borrowed the same amount from her father-in-law a few years later.

Taylor ran the company out of her house until it got its first large corporate order, which was from Neiman Marcus. In 1993, she used money from that to buy an old seed farm with two barns and a chicken coop in the northern Philadelphia suburb of Doylestown, Pennsylvania. She had the chicken coop knocked down and put up an office building for her company in its place.

At first, Christine Taylor Collection specialized in fabric-covered items, such as cushions, folding screens, and chairs used in displays in domestics departments. After a few years, Taylor realized she needed to branch out, and she created a line of wrought-iron items. She had them produced domestically, like her textile items, but as she continued diversifying, her US manufacturers couldn't keep pace, and she began using factories in China.

By 2006, Christine Taylor Collection was doing well enough for Taylor to relocate it to its present location, also in Doylestown, and open an office in Hong Kong. The company's new headquarters building was 22,000 square feet, as opposed to its predecessor's 1,600 square feet, and dramatically upped the company's overhead expenses, which previously were very low.

Still, Christine Taylor Collection kept chugging along, and Taylor kept using its profits to fuel its growth instead of putting some aside to use as a cushion for a bad year.

That didn't pose a problem until the company's retailer customers cut back on their orders. The cutbacks were the result of a triple whammy that began with a weak 2015 holiday season, continued with an abnormally warm first quarter that left them unable to move much of their cold-weather merchandise, and concluded with a cold and rainy second quarter that slowed their spring sales, too.

As a result, when July rolled around, instead of getting orders for its holiday display products, Christine Taylor Collection received apologetic phone calls from its customers' representatives explaining that their bosses were cutting their budgets in an effort to save money wherever possible, and so they'd have to cut back on their orders.

Her company operates in a small industry in which all the players know each other, so Taylor knew her competitors were facing the same problem. While she was glad her company hadn't lost market share, that didn't alleviate its financial situation. In November 2016, Taylor was expecting its revenue for the year to be $6 million, half of its 2015 figure, and thought it was poised to lose $1.4 million.

When initially interviewed, Taylor said that if she were able to borrow up to $1 million at 6 percent for Christine Taylor Collection, she would borrow the entire amount. But when push came to shove, she chose a different path and decided to sell her business. She no longer wanted to take the risk.

When I recently caught up with Taylor, she was thrilled with her decision to exit.

REFLECTION

What stage are you in in your business journey? Entrepreneurs often have more than one answer, but it's helpful to identify a primary one. Also, remember that how you answer today may be different from how you answered a year ago and from how you will answer a year from now.

And remember, your answer will impact the financing options you are considering.

CHAPTER 6

What Is Your Risk Tolerance?

How do we make borrowing decisions? Our historical experiences with risk and money often influence how we choose to finance our businesses today. We each think about risk differently, and often our opinions change over time. Typically, our opinions are based on how we grew up and what our experiences with money were like.

SOME IMPORTANT VOCABULARY

While money and risk clearly generate many feelings and emotions, your true feelings will rapidly become clear when you have to make tough choices while reviewing loan documents. Some key terms are important to describe and are defined as follows.

PERSONAL GUARANTEES

Banks and other lenders tend to want to work with more established businesses that have track records, viable business plans, and actual ongoing sales to report.

Don't take offense if lenders are skeptical about whether your dream business will succeed.

If you do secure a loan, you're going to pay more interest than an ongoing concern would pay (potentially much more), and there's a strong possibility that the lender will ask for a personal guarantee in exchange for a decent rate.

That personal guarantee very well may be a lien on your home; that's the case 95 percent of the time with federal SBA loans. With other lenders, it could be your home or some other valuable assets you possess.

That means you need to think about whether you are willing to make a personal guarantee before you apply for the loan—and probably even before you get into the entrepreneurial business since you'll be needing working capital at some point.

Consider it from the lender's perspective.

The lender wants affirmation that you believe in your business idea and have confidence in your ultimate success. What better way to express that confidence than by putting up personal possessions near and dear to you? It demonstrates that you are a responsible businessperson who intends to repay all obligations.

Since an entrepreneur's finances are often tied to their business, it makes sense for the lender to link them together.

Of course, read all the fine print to know what you're getting yourself into.

If possible, avoid having your spouse sign a personal guarantee, which enables you to protect assets that aren't jointly owned.

Also, try to limit the guarantee to a portion of the loan so you're not on the hook for the entire amount. Not all lenders will agree to this, but some will, depending upon your circumstances.

If there is more than one business owner or investor, spread the risk to each person in proportion to their ownership stake. Personal guarantee insurance is another option that can minimize risk.

For those who aren't willing to commit to a personal guarantee—and find themselves unable to get a loan—the best alternative is to find an equity partner.

LIENS

When business owners consider a loan, their primary concerns are generally things you would expect: What is the interest rate? How big is the loan? What will the monthly payments be?

But another issue often lurks in the background and gets overlooked: What liens will the lender take, and how will they affect the owner's ability to borrow in the future? Sometimes the answers to these questions can be devastating.

When a lender files a lien, it places them in a position where they can take the borrower's assets in case of default. Sometimes additional liens are filed by other creditors behind the first lender's lien—but these creditors assume subordinate positions and would be able to claim proceeds in a liquidation only after the holder of the first lien has been paid off.

Naturally, lenders prefer to be in the first lien position. If a lender does take a second or third lien position, the loan is riskier—and often requires a much higher interest rate. And that is why paying attention to the lien is critical. When you give up first lien position on some or all of your assets, you want to make sure that you are getting the money you need at the right price—because subsequent loans are likely to be either more expensive or impossible to obtain. Unfortunately, many entrepreneurs don't pay attention to this.

I once helped a rapidly growing client that had outgrown its line of credit with a bank. It was growing fast, but it was not profitable enough for the bank to extend more money. Instead, the company chose to take money from an accounts receivable factoring company. We made our client aware of the higher cost associated with factoring, but given the company's relatively high margins and growth prospects, the owner was willing to pay the higher price for faster access to capital.

As part of the process of setting up the factoring relationship, we learned that the company's current lender had placed a blanket lien against all assets of the business, including the accounts receivable. We worked with the client to evaluate the option of using some of the proceeds of factoring to pay off the existing bank line. The factoring arrangement still made sense, and our client made arrangements to pay off the existing line of credit at closing, at which time the bank would remove its lien on the receivables to be replaced by a new lien owned by the factoring company.

But as we moved toward closing, we were surprised to learn that the company had entered into a purchase-finance agreement for a small piece of equipment a few months earlier, and the equipment seller had placed a blanket lien on all of our client's assets, including its receivables. Without removing this lien, the transaction could not proceed because the factoring company, understandably, insisted on being in the first position on the asset they were lending against. Much to our surprise, the equipment company would not agree, and the client had to make the difficult decision to pay off the equipment loan with proceeds from the factoring agreement at a much higher rate and on less favorable terms.

We also recently helped a borrower who was operating two franchises and wanted to open a third. So far, this small franchisee has managed to build his business with only one loan—a fairly small SBA loan that he used to purchase a trailer truck to take to events.

While the loan represented only 20 percent of the amount needed for the new location, the business was now stuck because the new lender required a blanket first position lien, which the SBA would not accept. In this case, to proceed with the planned expansion, the client is likely to have to refinance his equipment at a higher rate with a lender that will take a lien only on the equipment.

I hope that these examples convey how critical it is to think through the lien and collateral requirements of your lender to make sure that when you're giving up first lien position on some or all of your assets, you're getting the best possible loan return.

WHAT IS YOUR RISK TOLERANCE?

We each have our own tolerance for risk—and it's a critical issue to consider as we think through debt, leverage, and growth.

Take a minute to think about your risk tolerance.

WHAT IS YOUR TOLERANCE FOR RISK?

Consider your answer to each of these questions and then total your score at the end:

> 1—Would not consider, no, never.
>
> 3—Would consider given a better understanding of the situation and the costs/benefits.
>
> 5—Would consider, am open to situation.

1. By providing a personal guarantee, you are able to obtain a larger credit facility, a lower interest rate, or other generally more favorable terms. Do you provide the personal guarantee?

   A: _____

2. Your business is doing well. It is growing organically each year, you have a solid management team in place, and cash flow and earnings are robust. You are faced with the opportunity to expand (add a new production line, acquire a competitor, expand into a new facility) but do not need to. However, the financing is available. Do you expand?

   A: _____

3. Your business is growing faster than your current lender can fund. You have the option of replacing the existing low-cost lender with a higher-interest accounts receivable factor. Do you replace the conventional financing source with the

higher-rate factor, understanding that otherwise you will have to slow down your growth? Consider your own specific growth situation (inventory, purchase orders, additional equipment).

A: _____

4. Are you willing to provide additional collateral (business or personal) in order to obtain the most appropriate funding structure for your business?

A: _____

5. You are facing a choice of paths for your company's future— which can happen to early-stage companies or anyone facing a significant change. Your options to address the issue have been narrowed down to two choices: (1) equity partner, or (2) financing. If you bring in a new equity partner, you may improve liquidity, resolve that issue, and/or improve your balance sheet, but you are now married to that new partner, and you have ceded partial control of your business. Or do you take the debt option, even if the cost of financing is high? It means greater control for you but greater financial risk. Assuming that the equity partner is lower risk and the debt option is higher risk, how do you proceed? (If you choose the equity route—give yourself a 1. If you choose the debt, give yourself a 5.)

A: _____

TOTAL SCORE: _____

SCORING

 5 to 12—RISK AVERSE: This is the most risk adverse of the profiles. You choose to take the more conservative paths that mitigate risk but also may limit growth and options. Your best financing sources are conventional lenders, or you may opt for self-financing or equity funding only. This is the least leveraged of the profiles.

 13 to 18—RISK NEUTRAL: You are open to risk when it is carefully balanced against the rewards. You may see opportunity in some higher-cost, but quicker or more tailored, financing while skewing toward more traditional sources.

 19 to 25—RISK FLEXIBLE: You are the intrepid entrepreneur willing to take risks knowing that they can lead to larger rewards. You may have the highest leverage of the profiles, but you seek to match financing to asset class and to understand the conditions that come along with each.

DOES YOUR SCORE SURPRISE YOU?

Whether or not it does, let's look at each group of entrepreneurs, starting with the risk averse.

But first, a surprising statistic. A study of 250 British entrepreneurs a few years ago reported that 52 percent described themselves as having risk-averse characteristics.

The author of *Entrepreneurship for the Rest of Us* wrote about risk aversion in *Forbes* a couple of years back. Paul B. Brown said, "Successful serial entrepreneurs adhere to the basic principles of risk management: If you're going to play in a game with uncertain outcomes, 1) don't pay/bet more than what you can expect as a return, and 2) don't pay/bet more than you can afford to lose."[1]

RISK AVERSE

Most risk-averse entrepreneurs would be hesitant to provide a personal guarantee in exchange for a lower interest rate, a larger credit facility, or other favorable terms. The idea of providing additional collateral to obtain the most appropriate funding structure for their business is out, too.

And they are not open to the idea of bringing in an equity partner—and giving up some control of the company.

That said, there are still some options.

Conventional lenders are probably going to be the best financing sources. Because the risk averse are likely to approach business

---

1 Paul B. Brown, "Hate Risk? You Could Be the Perfect Entrepreneur," *Forbes*, accessed September 1, 2013, https://www.forbes.com/sites/actiontrumpseverything/2013/09/01/hate-risk-you-could-be-the-perfect-entrepreneur/#66193a41300e.

conservatively, their overall financial practices may be best matched with SBA-approved lenders.

Another possibility (one that is among the top forms start-ups use for financing) is self-financing. This entails using your own money to invest in the company; personal assets are used as collateral for outside funding.

Some examples include securing a home-equity loan or home-equity line of credit (HELOC); borrowing against life insurance; using your Individual Retirement Account (IRA) for a short-term, interest-free loan; borrowing against investments and securities; or even using a credit card or personal savings.

These aren't the only options, but they give you an example of available funding sources that a risk-averse company can stomach.

RISK NEUTRAL

Now let's look at risk-neutral businesses.

Unlike the risk-averse companies, these entrepreneurs are open to risks, so long as they are balanced against the rewards. That means every option, taken in moderation, at least merits consideration.

While there's no way a risk-averse entrepreneur would provide a personal guarantee in exchange for things such as a lower interest rate or a larger credit facility, a risk-neutral entrepreneur would.

Now consider another possibility.

A client's business is growing organically at a solid pace, both cash flow and earnings are sound, and there's a strong management team in place.

A risk-averse company would be happy with the status quo and not touch a thing.

A risk-neutral entrepreneur might have greater aspirations and realize the opportunity to grow the business is too good to forgo.

That entrepreneur would consider taking advantage of available financing—remember, the company is doing well, so the terms are likely to be favorable—and expand. The money could go toward buying a new facility, establishing a new production line, acquiring a competitor, or committing money to research and development.

Meantime, the risk-neutral entrepreneur could switch lenders, especially if the business is growing faster than the existing bank can lend to it.

And while there's no chance a risk-averse entrepreneur would swap out a low-cost lender for something such as a higher-interest accounts receivable factor (even if it meant slowing growth), under the right circumstances a risk-neutral company would do exactly that. It would all depend on the situation and would involve issues such as inventory, purchase orders, and the need for additional equipment.

RISK FLEXIBLE

 Finally, let's examine risk-flexible companies—those organizations led by entrepreneurs committed to taking significant risks to yield much larger rewards.

Note: This only means they would consider any option. It doesn't mean that they're reckless. There must be a clear-cut reason and reward for them to make riskier choices.

That said, providing a personal guarantee to obtain a larger credit facility or a lower interest rate may well be a no-brainer for this kind of entrepreneur. A personal guarantee is an individual's legal promise to repay business debts.

Business guarantees, which are sort of the opposite of personal guarantees, could also come into play, especially with somewhat larger businesses. Those are credit card agreements that shift the responsibility for debts the business owner incurs to the business itself—helpful when the business owner's financials are a bit suspect.

Committing additional collateral to obtain the most appropriate funding structure for the business is also a possibility. This might include an entrepreneur placing a lien on their home—which means the lender could gain an interest in (or take outright) the borrower's home. Financiers appreciate those kinds of liens because they showcase an entrepreneur's confidence in his or her business.

The same holds true when the opportunity to obtain additional financing at favorable terms is presented—even if things already are going well. Risk-flexible entrepreneurs aren't the type to pass up opportunities.

Another possibility includes taking on an equity partner (or partners).

In summary, it should be noted that, while entrepreneurs can be lumped into three categories, each category has multiple problem-solving possibilities that can be employed. Finances are an ever-changing thing—and even entrepreneurs may alter their philosophies to some extent—so one-size-fits-all is never an option.

How is your risk tolerance impacting your growth plans?

DO YOU HAVE NO DEBT?

Sometimes we run across CEOs who have no debt, although they have had it in the past. Invariably, they report being happy, saying they have no worries and that managing their businesses is much easier without the threat of repayment hanging over their heads.

That's all well and good. And it's certainly better to be running a company with no debt than one that's drowning in it. But debt isn't invariably bad. In fact, executives at companies with no debt should be asking themselves three questions.

Is there a line of credit in place? Maybe you don't need credit at the moment, but having a line of credit for your business prepares you for the risks you're always facing. Fires that destroy your inventory don't announce themselves in advance. Competitors don't discuss new products that will make yours obsolete. Expensive equipment often gives no signs it's going to break. Having a credit line enables you to deal with all those potential problems. Also, remember that it's best to secure a line of credit when you don't need it. The fact that you have no debt should ensure a good rate. And remember that a credit line carries minimal risk because interest is charged only on the portion you use. There's no charge if you don't use the line.

Is your lack of debt hurting your growth prospects? Yes, you might be making a substantial amount of money, but wouldn't you like to make more? There's an old saying that if you aren't trying to move ahead, someone else is likely to run you over. Say a chief competitor of yours goes belly-up. Sure, you'll probably obtain some of its business by default, but by being aggressive, you can capture a much larger chunk. Getting a loan might enable you to hire some of its best employees, buy its inventory or other resources, or expand to markets you hadn't tapped before. In a different scenario, say you're presented with the opportunity to buy raw materials at a one-time incredibly low price. By using debt wisely, you can buy those materials and make it back—and then some—when your manufacturing costs plummet.

If you had more debt, could you make more money? While similar to the second question, there are some differences. Remember that investing in your company isn't a bad thing. Research and development costs money. So does expanding the sales force or the distribution network. Advertising, marketing, and public-relations campaigns don't come for free. In other words, it costs money to make money.

REFLECTION

Having no debt is a good thing, no doubt about it. But the well-planned, strategic use of debt can be far better, leading to much faster growth, higher profit margins, and a stronger bottom line.

Properly executed, debt is a strategic tool. Are you comfortable with the amount of debt and leverage you are currently deploying in your company? Is it time to consider becoming less comfortable—should you shake things up?

Our willingness to tolerate risk—whether in business or throughout life—dictates many of our decisions. Take the risk-tolerance test and identify whether you're risk averse, neutral, or tolerant. Did your score surprise you?

Your risk-tolerance score doesn't have to limit your opportunities for growth. There are many options for financing and expanding your current business model. Seek them out, and take the time to explore different options and the guarantees they involve.

PROFILE OF A RISK-AVERSE ENTREPRENEUR: HARTH BUILDERS

G regory Harth's father, Allyn, started Harth Builders in 1996 as a retirement project. "The darned thing took off. And as a result, he invited me to join him every year for the first eight years, and finally I joined him in 2003," he said.

At the time, the home-remodeling company, based in the northern Philadelphia suburb of Spring House, had annual revenue of $700,000 and employed Harth, his father, and a part-time office manager.

Since then, the company has grown its revenue 15 percent per year and was on pace to post a profit on revenue of $6.5 million in 2016. It now employs thirty-two people and has changed its structure to an S corporation owned solely by Harth, its president, with his father as CEO.

Given all that, you might think that if Harth were given $1 million that he could divide between a mutual fund and his company, he'd put all the money in his company. If so, you'd be wrong. Harth would put only 45 percent of the $1 million into Harth Builders.

One reason is he has two daughters, ages six and three, and while he thinks an investment in his company would outperform an investment in a mutual fund, he is more risk averse as a forty-three-year-old father than he was as a younger man.

Another is that even though Harth Builders has become one of the *Philadelphia Business Journal*'s fastest-growing companies, Harth has always treated it as a vehicle for him to take cash out of, in addition to a growth asset. Harth's goal for the company is to enable it to pay him 10 percent of its revenue, be viable, and grow 15 percent per year. Taking out that amount would enable him to realize his goal of being financially independent by fifty-five. "That means I can choose to go to work as opposed to having to go to work."

Although Harth has ambitious wealth goals for himself, they aren't at the expense of his workers. He said that after he achieved his goal of making 10 percent of the company's revenue in 2015, he felt guilty about making too much, so he implemented a 20 percent profit-sharing plan for Harth Builders' employees. He also gives employees a say in how the company is run via the Open-Book Management process described by Jack Stack in his original book *The Great Game of Business.*

The balance Harth strikes between growing his company and keeping his family secure puts him between being a grower and a glider.

So far, Harth Builders has achieved its growth as a design-build remodeling firm, which employs architects and interior designers to help its customers figure out what they can achieve within their budgets. "We work on a fixed-price contract, and we help bring people's dreams to life," he said.

The company has specialized in extensive renovations, rather than what Harth called "pull and replace." The reason, he said, is the changes in how people live, which their homes reflect. Homes today differ from their counterparts thirty years ago in more than just the appliances, plumbing, and lighting fixtures they contain, so remodeling them entails redesigning them as much as, if not more than, replacing the outdated equipment in them.

To achieve the growth Harth wants his business to obtain, he has had the company branch out into new construction, building a development of eleven carriage homes in Spring House that can bring in $11 million over two years. Still, Harth stated that if he could borrow up to $1 million for his business at 6 percent, he would take only half of it. "There are only so many new initiatives I can pursue with added capital without growing the company too fast," he said.

REFLECTION

Harth is one of the most conservative entrepreneurs we have profiled so far. His perspective has changed over time, as is often the case.

If you were in Harth's shoes, would you make the same decisions he is making? What can you learn from his example?

CHAPTER 7

What Are Your Growth Aspirations?

A t different stages of our entrepreneurial journeys, we think about growth and goals differently.

We might call some goals *stretch goals*—meaning they require us to extend to our furthest limits. In other words, a stretch goal is something that goes a bit beyond what a business might consider a reasonable expectation. They are challenging, but they're not beyond the realm of possibility, either.

And because many entrepreneurs aren't aware of the myriad funding options available to them, those stretch goals sometimes do become attainable.

AN EXAMPLE

I once asked a group of entrepreneurs to list their three-year goals for their businesses. One woman had a consulting firm that was annually generating revenue of $2 million and $350,000 of earnings before interest, taxes, depreciation, and amortization (EBITDA). She said she wanted to double its revenue.

"That's great," I said. "What's it going to take for you to do that?" She said she'd have to install a management team, so I asked what that would cost, and she said $350,000 before the team started to pay for itself. When I prodded her about why she hadn't hired a management team, she responded, understandably, that she wanted to do better than break even for a year.

I said, "Have you thought about borrowing money from the SBA at 6.5 percent?" The loan would amortize over ten years, and she'd have a monthly payment of $3,600 and no prepayment penalty.

She was dumbfounded. That had never occurred to her, even though it was relatively safe. Her annual obligation would be $43,200, which was only 12 percent of her EBITDA. So even if the management team she hired turned out to be a disaster and she had to get rid of it, she'd be able not only to keep making the payments on the loan but also to pay it off early.

Like most business owners, she was managing her company off its income statement rather than its balance sheet. As a result, she could only think of financing its growth with its revenues, rather than with its assets.

She was lucky that she had choices.

Some entrepreneurs can't use debt to fund their business's expansion because the company doesn't generate enough cash to enable them to make the payments on it. Others shouldn't use debt because the returns their business can earn on borrowed money are less than the interest rates on any loans they can get. Still, for many entrepreneurs looking to grow their companies, debt is an option they can and should consider.

WHAT IS YOUR STRETCH GOAL?

Look three years ahead in conducting this exercise. That time span allows room for both growth and projections.

MY STRETCH GOAL FOR MY BUSINESS IN THREE YEARS IS:

	Last Year	In Three Years	% Change	Annual Change
Revenue				
EBITDA				

I am being held back by:

a. _____

b. _____

c. _____

Examples: Management Team, Equipment, Capital, New Products, Acquisition Targets, etc.

The estimated capital infusion I need to accomplish my goals is:

$ \underline{\hspace{10cm}}

Remember that EBITDA measures the operating performance of a company. "Essentially, it's a way to evaluate a company's performance without having to factor in financing decisions, accounting decisions or tax environments," according to investinganswers. com[1]. (This website also walks you through the actual calibration.)

Some examples of what might be holding you back could include a weak management team, the need for new (or additional) equipment, limited capital, the lack of new products, or few acquisition targets that make sense. These are just a handful of possibilities; the number of hindrances is theoretically unlimited.

Finally, ask about the estimated capital infusion the company would need to accomplish its goals.

Calculating the percentage increase is fairly simple. The first step is to determine the difference of the two numbers you are comparing. Second, you divide the increase by the original number. Finally, you multiply this number by 100.

Once you have calculated your overall percentage change, go one step further and divide it by three to determine your annual growth rate.

---

1   "Earnings Before Interest, Tax, Depreciation and Amortization," *InvestingAnswers.com,* accessed October 5, 2017, http://www.investinganswers. com/financial-dictionary/financial-statement-analysis/earnings-interest-tax-depreciation-and-amortizatio.

SOME DATA

It's worth noting that your stretch goals may not have to be that big of a stretch, according to data from Sageworks (www.sageworks. com), a financial information company.

For example, Sageworks examined more than 650,000 retail companies in the United States and noted that "small retailers continued to improve sales, but their sales increases were flat to slightly lower than in previous years."[1]

In addition, debt to EBITDA stayed consistently between 6 and 7 percent.

Net profit growth, however, was higher, ranging from an annual rate of about 14 percent to, in three separate years, about 18 percent.

Other fields performed better, but not at extreme rates.

In the world of health care and social assistance, growth rates landed in a range of anywhere from 5.5 percent to 7.5 percent, while net profit margins consistently checked in at about 8.5 percent.

Debt to EBITDA remained constant each year between 3 and 4 percent, while net profit growth fluctuated between 10.5 percent and 17 percent.

Overall, in 2015, businesses with less than $5 million in annual revenue enjoyed annual sales growth of 7.8 percent, according to Sageworks, while net profit margins were 7.5 percent.

---

1 Sageworks Stats, "The State of U.S. Small Businesses Entering 2016," *Forbes*, accessed January 17, 2016, https://www.forbes.com/sites/ sageworks/2016/01/17/the-state-of-u-s-small-businesses-entering- 2016/#62599dac2f0b.

The point seems clear: A stretch goal doesn't have to be an outlandish reach and may well be within your grasp.

WHAT KIND OF STRETCHER ARE YOU?

Entrepreneurs have different growth ambitions. This often depends on what stage their business is in, their industry, and their appetite for risk. Here are some classifications to consider.

CONSERVATIVE STRETCHERS

 The most cautious businesses (and often the most mature) strive for growth of 5 percent per year. We might classify these entrepreneurs as extreme tortoises. They are happy with very slow and steady growth.

MODERATE STRETCHERS

 Moderate Stretchers push for growth rates between 5 and 15 percent per year. They want to keep moving up the ladder, but at a steady pace.

AGGRESSIVE STRETCHERS

Aggressive Stretchers are willing to push hard and push for growth between 15 and 25 percent per year. At these rates, you have to be willing to plan and invest ahead of the curve.

ROCKET-SHIP STRETCHERS

These entrepreneurs push for annual growth rates north of 25 percent. If you want to grow at these rates, prepare to potentially break things, and hold on for a crazy ride.

REFLECTION

What is your stretch goal—the number you aspire to that will take a bit of reach and imagination? It doesn't have to be outlandish.

Now think about the ingredients you will need to bake your new cake—or to meet your goals. What are you missing, and what is holding you back?

PROFILE OF A ROCKET-SHIP STRETCHER:
DAZADI

G iven the choice of investing all or part of $1 million into his business—or choosing the relative safety of mutual-fund investing—Jason Boyce didn't hesitate. He'd put it all in his business, Dazadi.

The name Dazadi is taken from the words *audacity* and *tzadik,* a Hebrew word for a righteous person. While the company is based in Calabasas, California, it's an internet-only seller of recreational and fitness products for the home. That includes everything from exercise bikes, elliptical trainers, and rowing machines to billiards tables, pinball machines, photo booths, patio furniture, saunas, and aboveground swimming pools. That's his business . . . and business is good.

"E-commerce is exploding, and we're poised to continue growing for some time," said Boyce, the company's CEO and cofounder.

While he didn't have an exact number on the return he'd get from a $1 million investment in Dazadi, Boyce said, "It's a hell of a lot more than the 8 to 10 percent I'd get from a mutual fund."

Boyce said he would use the money to give Dazadi the type of infrastructure required to sustain high growth as well as inventory. "Adding the right kind of inventory adds revenue and gross margin, while building out infrastructure supports that growth," he said.

That's important because Boyce knows he's competing against both niche retailers and general behemoths such as Amazon.com, Wayfair, and Walmart. And the number of competitors is growing. "The biggest increase in competitors in the last year or two have been Chinese competitors selling direct into the United States via their own websites and the online marketplaces like Amazon," Boyce said, noting that Dazadi is also expanding. "Next year, we'll start selling products in the EU. We also plan to expand our backyard and patio category of products as well. E-commerce in general is a rising tide of business, so it's nice to be part of that and have that built-in growth. However, we're very conscious about growth rates and are actively planning to keep them going."

If Boyce could borrow up to $1 million for Dazadi at 6 percent, he said he'd borrow the full amount—under one condition: "Six percent is a relatively good rate, but it would have to be fixed, as interest rates are expected to rise in the coming years."

Boyce noted that Dazadi has used financing in the past to cover losses during lean times, but the ongoing growth now allows the company to use financing to increase its inventory.

Dazadi was founded in May 2002 and is owned by Boyce (in his first business venture after leaving the marine corps), his two brothers, and four private investors. The company was on track to generate about $25 million in revenue in 2016 and is profitable and continues to grow.

"We have a sales goal of reaching $100 million in revenue by the end of 2020. After that, who knows? As long as we're still able to offer compelling products and service, we may continue adding sales categories and apply our lessons learned selling current items to additional products. It's not out of the question to think that one day Dazadi could be a $1 billion company," Boyce said.

That projection, plus what he'd do if he were given or could borrow $1 million, makes Boyce a full-fledged grower.

Dazadi used to have a small retail presence solely to get some vendors to sell their products, but as e-commerce continues to grow, fewer vendors require a retail store. Still, Boyce didn't rule out potentially opening seasonal pop-up stores in the future. For now, though, it's all about e-commerce.

"I feel like we're creating something. Even though e-commerce has been done, it's still in its infancy, and learning and adapting to this rapidly changing environment is a lot of fun. It can get frustrating at times to be forced to constantly be adapting to new methods of selling, but it really keeps things interesting," he said.

REFLECTION

Boyce's answer has a twist. He would borrow the money only at a fixed interest rate. Borrowing the money is one thing, but the terms of the loan are critical.

Have you recently reviewed your debt to look at the fixed and variable interest rate loans? Do you have any fixed rates that will soon reset? It's important to check in on these regularly.

CHAPTER 8

Should You Get a Loan to Grow?

Let's say you want to borrow more money. A lot of variables and tools go into building a business: people, product, service levels, marketing message, culture, and financing, just to name a few.

In the middle of the ever-flowing tide of business is another question that can often be the key to a lot of issues: Are you over-leveraged or underleveraged? Some companies have borrowed their maximum. Even if they wanted to, borrowing more money and using it to expand or grow is not an option. They have leveraged their cash flow or collateral, and they have no more alternatives.

Many companies are in the opposite situation: They are under-leveraged. If they wanted to inject capital onto their balance sheet, they have plenty of opportunities to do so.

If you are underleveraged, there are a few key questions to ask.

First, how much money could you borrow, at what rates, and over what terms? If you were to maximize your leverage or take full advantage of the cash flow or assets your company has built, how much money could you get? Then you need to ask yourself two questions: What would you do with the money, and do the potential benefits outweigh the risks?

The goal of this exercise is not to leverage yourself to the hilt. The intent is to start managing your business based on your balance sheet instead of your income statement.

If you can borrow more money and you have a good idea what you can do with it, come up with three simple scenarios.

What is the worst that could happen? If the investment is a disaster and doesn't generate incremental revenue, what would happen to your cash flow as you pay off the debt? We'll call this the worst-case scenario.

The other side of the coin is the home-run scenario. If everything worked out perfectly, how much incremental profit would you generate, and how quickly could you pay down the debt? This is the best-case scenario.

The third scenario is something in the middle, which we'll call the base scenario.

Sometimes working through this exercise can unlock whole new ways to think about offensively growing your business.

Just because you *can* get debt to grow your business doesn't mean you *should*. To see if taking out a loan to finance your company's growth makes sense, you need to determine whether your proposed investment will generate enough money to pay off the loan and increase your profits.

Let's consider an entrepreneur with a profitable company that currently makes $1 million in annual revenue. She thinks her company is poised for rapid growth and just needs a little boost to its sales and marketing efforts to begin expanding rapidly. And she thinks she can give it that boost by doubling the size of both her sales and marketing departments from one to two people. This would enable the employees she currently has to begin thinking strategically and not simply fulfill the company's sales and marketing duties. With benefits, the two new hires will cost her company $150,000 per year. She thinks the positions will pay for themselves after a short while but is worried about how much they will cost until they do.

She is a candidate for a ten-year SBA loan for $75,000, half the cost of the new sales and marketing employees' salaries and benefits in their first year, at a rate of 6.5 percent. To see if she should get the loan, let's consider three scenarios and see how each would affect her company in one year.

WORST-CASE SCENARIO

The first is the worst-case scenario. In it, adding the positions doesn't bring in any additional sales.

Since the loan payment amounts to $851.61 per month and the employees' monthly cost is $12,500, the entrepreneur's company would lose $160,219.32 on the positions in twelve months.

Worst-Case Scenario: $0/month incremental sales		Monthly	Yearly
Incremental sales		$0.00	$0.00
Salaries and benefits		-$12,500.00	-$150,000.00
Amortization		-$851.61	-$10,219.32
Net cash flow		-$13,351.61	-$160,219.32
ROI with debt	-213.6%		
ROI without debt	-100.0%		
Loan payback	10 years		

That's not good, but there are some mitigating factors:

This scenario is improbable. Unless the employees are comatose, adding them probably would bring in some extra revenue.

Almost all the loss is due to the new employees' salaries and benefits. The loan payments are relatively cheap.

Since the loan paid for six months of the new employees' salaries and benefits, the company would be out only $85,219.32, a year's loan payments ($10,219.32) and half a year of the new employees' salary and benefits ($75,000).

If the new staff are such a disaster that our entrepreneur must fire them after a year, her company would be out a total of $177,193.20 ($75,000 in salaries and benefits and $102,193.20 in loan payments) over ten years, assuming it doesn't pay off the loan early. That's only 1.8 percent of its total revenue over the term of the loan.

BASE SCENARIO

Now, let's look at the scenario the entrepreneur thinks is most likely to happen. In it, adding the positions brings in $15,000 per month in additional sales.

Here, as you can see from the table that follows, the new employees are paying for themselves from the first month, bringing in sales that are more than the total of their cost and the loan payments. At this rate, the loan payback period, the amount of time it would take for the company to recoup the $75,000 it borrowed (assuming it sets aside all yearly net cash flow generated by the new employees), would be about three years and ten months.

Base Scenario: $15,000/month incremental sales		Monthly	Yearly
Incremental sales		$15,000.00	$180,000.00
Salaries and benefits		-$12,500.00	-$150,000.00
Amortization		-$851.61	-$10,219.32
Net cash flow		$1,648.39	$19,780.68
ROI with debt	26.4%		
ROI without debt	20.0%		
Loan payback	< 4 years		

BEST-CASE SCENARIO

We've saved the best for last. In this scenario, adding the two new employees enables our entrepreneur's company to bring in an additional $25,000 per month.

As that's $300,000 per year and the company is paying the new employees only $150,000 per year, if our entrepreneur were guaranteed that this scenario would occur, she likely wouldn't have to take out a loan at all. But if she did borrow $75,000 for ten years at 6.5 percent, the net cash flow generated by the new employees would enable the company to recoup the loan amount in less than a year.

The tables presented here include calculations of the monthly payment the company would have to make on the loan and the amount of time in which the net cash flow generated by hiring the new employees would cover the loan amount. Explaining how to calculate the monthly debt payment would take up too much space here, but you can find amortization tables online that do it for you. The loan payback period is easy to calculate. Divide $75,000, the amount of the loan taken out to help pay for the new employees, by the annual net cash flow that hiring them produces.

Best-Case Scenario: $25,000/ month incremental sales		Monthly	Yearly
Incremental sales		$25,000.00	$300,000.00
Salaries and benefits		-$12,500.00	-$150,000.00
Amortization		-$851.61	-$10,219.32
Net cash flow		$11,648.39	$139,780.68
ROI with debt	186.4%		
ROI without debt	100.0%		
Loan payback	< 1 year		

The tables also contain two figures that demonstrate the pluses and minuses of borrowing money and show why doing so gives you what is called leverage. The numbers are the return on investment (ROI) with and without the loan, or with and without debt.

ROI is simple to calculate. These tables are for one year, so it amounts to the total cash flow generated by the new employees in a year divided by the amount that the entrepreneur's company invests in them in the same period.

In all scenarios, the company puts up $75,000 of its own money to pay half the new employees' salaries and benefits for one year and borrows $75,000 to pay the other half. That means it has an equity investment of $75,000 in the employees. In the worst-case scenario, the employees produce no additional revenue, so they generate a negative cash flow of $160,219.32, the total of their cost in salaries and benefits ($150,000) plus one year's payments on the loan ($10,219.32). Dividing that by $75,000 equals a negative 2.136, meaning the ROI is –213.6 percent.

Let's suppose, however, that our entrepreneur doesn't have her company borrow money to help fund the first year's salaries and benefits for the two new employees, and instead the company pays the $150,000 itself. In that case, in the worst-case scenario, the company has made an equity investment of $150,000 to pay for the employees. But also, because it doesn't borrow any money, it doesn't have any loan payments, so its negative cash flow when the employees don't generate any new revenue is only $150,000. Dividing that by the equity investment of $150,000 equals –1. That means the ROI is –100 percent. That's less than –213.6

percent, so our entrepreneur's company does better in the first scenario by not borrowing money.

Now let's look at the base scenario. In it, the two new employees enable our entrepreneur's company to bring in an additional $15,000 per month, or $180,000 per year. When the company takes out a $75,000 loan to help pay their salaries and benefits, it has loan payments of $10,219.32 per year. That amount plus their annual $150,000 in wages and benefits means their total cost is $160,219.32 per year. Subtracting that from the extra $180,000 per year they bring in means the net cash flow they produce is $19,780.68. Dividing that by the $75,000 equity investment that our entrepreneur's company made to help fund their costs produces a result of 0.264, an ROI of 26.4 percent.

Suppose again that our entrepreneur doesn't have her company borrow money to help fund the first year's salaries and benefits for the two new employees, and instead the company pays the $150,000 itself. That means the net cash flow they generate is $180,000 minus $150,000, or $30,000. That's higher than the net cash flow when the company uses debt to help fund its positions because it doesn't include loan payments. The equity investment is also higher—$150,000 as compared to $75,000—because the company hasn't taken out a loan to fund half of the employees' costs. The result is that the ROI is $30,000 divided by $150,000, which is 0.2 or 20 percent, slightly lower than the 26.4 percent ROI that our entrepreneur generates using debt to pay for half of the employees' costs.

As you can see, in the worst-case scenario, our entrepreneur fares worse by borrowing money. If you use it to fund a project that loses money, you generate a lower ROI than you would have if you had not used debt to fund the project. At the same time, however, if you use debt to fund a profitable project, you can generate a greater ROI than you could have without using debt, as the base scenario shows. The reason is that the debt enables you to put less equity in the project, making the denominator in the ROI calculation smaller, which makes the result of the calculation a bigger number. If that figure is negative because the project lost money, then you have a worse ROI with debt than without it. If the number is positive because the project made money, you have a better ROI with debt than without it.

Therefore, taking on debt is called adding leverage. Doing it enables you to make smaller equity investments in projects, which makes their ROIs more extreme. But as we can see from the previous scenarios, leverage can cut both ways. Not only can it increase the positive ROI on a successful project, but it can also increase the negative ROI on an unsuccessful project. That's another thing to think about when you're considering taking out a loan.

In our example, adding the new sales and marketing people isn't completely a no-brainer for our entrepreneur, as there's a chance the new employees might never generate any cash flow for her company. But since the payments on the loan she's getting to finance half of their first year's salaries are relatively small, and the loan payback period in the base scenario is less than the term of the loan, the additions look like a safe bet.

If you can forecast the cash flow generated by an action you're considering having your company take, you can see if getting a loan to finance it makes sense. Of course, there are other things to consider, such as your current debt load and overall situation. The other factors may prohibit your company from getting a loan or cause you to feel that taking on additional debt would be too risky. But many times you won't know if something's worth financing unless you crunch the numbers. And since all that costs is your time, it's almost always worth doing.

REFLECTION

Are you considering taking on debt? Slow down before you speed up.

Run the numbers! Just because you can get financing (take on debt) to grow your business doesn't mean you should. To see if taking out a loan makes sense, you need to determine whether your proposed investment will generate enough money to pay off the loan and increase your profits. Crunch the numbers and consider worst-case, base, and best-case scenarios. Leverage can cut both ways—greatly improving ROI on successful projects and cutting drastically into ROI on projects that fail.

CHAPTER 9

Valuable Lessons in the Hunt for Money

The best advice that I can give anyone hunting for money is to get organized early, do your research, identify your targets for financing, and pursue them in a focused and methodical way. As entrepreneurs, we often try throwing as much as we can against the wall to see what sticks. But when it comes to looking for money, this approach can consume time and is unlikely to end happily. Still, I see it all the time.

Imagine a biotechnology company that spends six months trying to pitch nearly every internet investor in the country. Or the owner of a start-up who networks only with lenders who require businesses to be profitable and to have been in business for at least two years. Imagine a loan application submitted with financial statements that have fundamental mistakes in them or are months behind. Or consider a business plan to raise investment money that was too poorly written to be understood. I know it sounds silly, but again, I see these kinds of mistakes all of the time.

One of the biggest mistakes that we see is that owners try to raise too much money. They think about how much money they need for the next several years instead of what they need to make real progress this year. In those situations, we often advise owners to take a cold shower and call us in the morning. If you're looking for a loan, you need sufficient collateral and cash flow to cover the debt.

The market for capital is inefficient, and in many cases results in gridlock for entrepreneurs, lenders, and investors. The smartest thing owners can do is to make sure they understand how the process works. You should figure out how much money you need and what the best loan or equity solution will be for you. Find an advisor or mentor you trust, one who has been around the block before. Understand what documents your lender or investor will demand, and make sure you have them together before you begin your search. Check your personal and business credit scores and make sure they are in order.

DEBT VS. EQUITY?

I have always been a big proponent of the principle that, whatever stage a company is in, when there is a need for capital, it is wise to consider both debt and equity alternatives and then decide which is best for you.

I have an inherit bias toward debt. It's almost always cheaper than equity if things work out as planned, and it allows the entrepreneur to stay in control of their company and avoid dilution.

There are three scenarios in which it's better to take on equity instead of debt:

1. If the company needs more money and has maximized its borrowing capacity.

2. If the CEO/entrepreneur feels that they have maxed out on the personal risk they are willing to take with the company and want to take some chips off the table.

3. If there is an investor who brings significant strategic value to the business (more than money), someone who you feel can help grow and support the business that you want to build.

Nonetheless, I offer two cautionary notes.

- There is probably a way to do what you want to do with a lot less money than you think. Challenge your assumptions hard and think through different scenarios.

- If you are courting an investor, think of the partnership like a marriage. Don't fall for the Shark Tank myth of love at first sight. Have serious conversations with the investor about the business you want to build, and discuss good and bad scenarios and how you would each respond to them.

Remember that when you take on a loan, you're obligating yourself to pay it back. And when you take on an investor, you effectively just got married for the life of your company. This decision is worth a lot of thought and consideration.

EQUITY INVESTMENT

Equity investment is when a business raises money by selling interests in the company. Investors, who could be as close to you as friends or family or as removed as angel investors or venture capitalists, take a percentage of your company when they agree to fund the business.

With equity financing, the investor is on the hook for the majority of the risk. If your business fails, you do not have to pay the investor back the money. No out-of-pocket payments means that you will also have more cash on hand to invest in the business up front; this is a huge relief for start-ups or companies that are just starting to turn profits and gain market leverage.

However, the downside of equity financing is enough for many entrepreneurs to shy away from this option. Understandably, investors in your company will share your profits and benefit from your successes. Since you will no longer be the sole owner, you will reap a smaller portion of the rewards for your hard work, a hard pill to swallow when the time comes to pay your investors.

In addition to giving up some of your future profits, you're also giving up some control of your company when you bring on investors. Before making decisions that will affect your business, you'll need to consult with your shareholders and keep them abreast of company actions.

DEBT

Just like taking out a loan for a car or a mortgage for a home, taking on debt for a business involves borrowing money to be repaid to a lender, plus interest. Businesses may be eligible for an SBA-backed loan, a private loan, a line of credit from a bank, or a personal loan from friends or family.

Unlike with equity financing, the lender in a debt financing arrangement has no control over your business. Once you have paid a loan back, the obligation is over. A creditor is entitled to the agreed-upon principal plus interest of the loan, not any future profits of the company.

Other advantages of debt are that interest paid on the debt is tax deductible, and the regularity of debt payments makes them easy to forecast and plan for out of monthly cash flow (in comparison to fluctuating investor obligations).

The disadvantages of debt financing are likely well known to any business owner who also has personal debt. Loan payments must be paid back on time, or the consequences can be severe for your business. By taking on debt, you are taking the risk that your company will not be able to pay back the loan.

Many business owners find themselves in a situation where debt payments hamper their ability to grow or stretch their funds too thin.

Although you won't need to give up control of your company with debt financing, you will need to pledge certain assets of the company as collateral and will often be required to offer up a personal guarantee.

LENDING IS A TWO-WAY RELATIONSHIP

Remember that when you're speaking to a potential investor or lender, you're entering a two-way relationship. They are investing or lending to make money. Just as they are interviewing you, you should do the same. How many investments have they made in the last year? If it's a loan officer you're talking to, how many loans have they made? What is their approval rate in the organization? Who will be making the final decision, and how much influence will your loan officer have on that person?

Once you've figured out where your company fits into the ecosystem, you really can't fight gravity. If you are eligible for a particular type of loan, it's unlikely that you are going to be able to twist a lender's arm into offering you a more favorable type of loan. The first loan you will be offered will have certain pricing and conditions associated with the risk the lender is taking. Once the bank has made this calculation, it rarely changes.

That said, it's important to remember that the type of loan your company is eligible for today could well change six months or a year from now. Companies change and evolve, and so do credit markets. Reviewing your loans on an annual basis is important. Some entrepreneurs get stuck because they think the loan they pick will last forever.

Once you've nailed down your loan type and pricing, you should step back and ask yourself questions like, "Will this loan allow me to focus on growing my business and making it more profitable?" and "Will I stop lying awake at night worrying about cash flow?" If both of the answers to these questions are yes, it's probably worth taking the loan.

I once worked with an electronics distributor who tried to fight gravity. Because the business shrank by 50 percent during the recession, its bank—even though the company stayed profitable—decided to call the line of credit. Since then, the distributor has been slowly paying down the credit line and holding on for dear life. In the last three months, it has twice needed to take emergency financing in the form of expensive merchant cash advance loans.

What the company desperately needs to do is to pay off the line of credit—and move to a factor. While the factor will be more expensive, it will lend the distributor all the working capital it needs. As a result, the owner will be able to sleep at night and focus on getting the company back to pre-recession levels. At that point, there will be no problem going back to a bank and getting a new line of credit.

We have another client who has a high-end used car business that owns its real estate. It has been banking with the same bank for seven years where it has a floor-plan line of credit (against retail inventory) and a real estate loan. But the bank was sold, and the new parent company won't do floor-plan lines anymore. In today's credit market, finding a floor-plan lender for used cars can be all but impossible. We managed to find one for our client, but he wouldn't accept the terms. He is trying to fight gravity, and it will catch up with him eventually.

It's not enough to understand your own business—you also have to understand credit markets and where you fit into them. And most of all, you have to know that they keep changing.

THE PATH TO BANKABILITY

Every company that chooses debt should reach the point where they are bankable through an SBA-backed loan or another traditional bank loan. If a company is considered bankable—that is, they meet all the criteria necessary to receive financing through an FDIC-insured bank—they've earned the right to get the cheapest loans that will give them the best opportunities to grow and create jobs.

That being said, I am not naïve enough to think that every company is bankable: In fact, most are not.

In cases when a company is non-bankable, its officers should choose financing instruments that increase their chances of being approved for a traditional bank loan.

While small businesses work toward this goal, it's likely that they will pay more for capital through alternative loans. However, don't get stuck in the land mines of alternative lending or be forced into endless renewals.

It's important to always treat borrowed money as a means to an end. The end for some businesses will be to pay off the loan. In many other cases, however, the end is becoming bankable and entering into an affordable FDIC-insured bank loan.

PROFILE: SKYLINE ATTRACTIONS

Consider Skyline Attractions' path to bankability.

Jeff Pike has wanted to design roller coasters since he was eight years old. For the past three years, he's been one of four partners in Skyline Attractions, an Orlando maker of innovative amusement-park rides. As a result, you'd think that if he were offered $1 million to divide between his company and a mutual fund, he'd put it all in his company.

He would, if he were single and childless. But with a wife and four children living in a rented home that's much smaller than the one his family owned before he left Great Coasters International to cofound Skyline Attractions, he felt he had to make a different decision. "I would probably take $900,000 of that and put it in the business. I'd put $100,000 in the mutual fund only because I've got the four kids, and it would be nice to maintain some amount of security for the kids until they're eighteen," he said.

Pike said he would expect a return of 5 percent from the mutual fund. In Skyline Attractions, he said, "I believe we could turn that $900,000 into several million dollars in the next couple years."

In part, he holds that belief because of a roller coaster the company is developing called Skywarp. On it, according to the Skyline Attractions website, "Thrill-seekers twist sideways and upside-down as they accelerate through twin Immelmann inversions!"

At the moment, Skyline Attractions only has enough money to build prototypes of the parts of Skywarp that its customers have the most questions about. The $900,000 wouldn't allow the company to build a complete prototype, but it would enable Skyline Attractions to construct a more complete one than it can now.

That, Pike said, would enable the company to cut Skywarp's sales cycle from two to three years down to one. As a result, instead of being able to have the first Skywarp open in 2018, Skyline Attractions would have been able to introduce it in 2017.

Not surprisingly, given his view of his company's prospects, Pike said that if he could borrow up to $1 million at 6 percent, he would take a loan out for the whole amount. That makes him a grower, albeit one with some reservations; if he were given $1 million to divide between Skyline Attractions and a mutual fund, he'd commit only 90 percent of it to the company.

Financing has been an issue for Skyline Attractions since its inception. For example, the company's first product line was GamesURide, which consists of two rides with elements of midway games: Strike-U-Up and Spin-U-Win. Pike said he and Skyline Attractions' three other partners, Chris Gray, Evan Souliere, and Bill Wydra, spent all their money and took on a little debt to get GamesURide ready for the International Association of Amusement Parks and Attractions' 2013 trade show.

Their rides went over well, with Strike-U-Up garnering a coveted Brass Ring Award for innovation in the industry, but, as is often the case, no park wanted to be the first to buy either GamesURide machine.

"Everybody's comment was, 'I can't wait to buy one as soon as somebody else buys one, and we'll see how it works out,'" Pike said.

With no buyers out of the gate, Pike and his partners began trying to work out deals to get GamesURide machines into parks. They reached a tentative deal with a large, nationally recognized chain of parks, under which the chain would lease six machines for two years with an option to buy them, but Pike said they couldn't get reasonable financing to build the units.

"We presented it to a couple of lenders, and they're like, 'No way!'" he said.

There are lenders that specialize in ride financing, but Pike said they usually finance only rides they know are popular so they can get the rides placed elsewhere or resell them if the rides have to be repossessed.

Skyline Attractions didn't sell any rides its first year in existence, but in its second year it got a GamesURide machine into Six Flags over Georgia on a revenue-sharing agreement, which started generating some cash. The company also has done well with a GamesURide machine it has operated at different venues, including Holiday World in Santa Claus, Indiana, and multiple events in California.

Prior to starting Skyline Attractions, Pike, Gray, and Souliere worked together at Great Coasters International, a roller-coaster maker based in Sunbury, Pennsylvania. They liked the company, but its focus was on building wooden roller coasters, and after awhile they wanted to do something more innovative. "We kind of collectively decided it was time to put our knowledge to the test," he said.

The three joined with Wydra, who had built coaster trains for Great Coasters International. Their plan was to get some

GamesURide machines into the market and then ramp up Skyline Attractions' manufacturing. But when they couldn't sell the machines, they switched their focus and began talking to potential customers to see what the customers were looking for.

They learned there was a market for kiddie rides built in the United States, came up with concepts for three such rides, pitched them to a potential customer in Florida, and sold one called Crazy Couch, which is like a giant sofa that moves up and down and side to side. Their efforts earned Skyline Attractions another Brass Ring Award, this time for the most innovative new kiddie ride. They since have sold two more Crazy Couches, and Pike said they expect to sell an additional dozen over the next year or so.

That won't make Pike and his partners rich, but Pike said it will allow them to focus on their true love, roller coasters. Skyline Attractions recently introduced Skywarp at a trade show. Pike said it was well received, and the company anticipates selling several. Pike said Skyline Attractions' ultimate goal is to operate its own amusement park, filled largely with its own rides.

The Mack family, which had been building roller coasters since 1921, opened its own park in Germany in 1975. Called Europa-Park, it won TripAdvisor's Travelers' Choice Award as Europe's most popular theme park in 2016 and won *Amusement Today's* Golden Ticket Award for being the Best Theme Park Worldwide in 2014, 2015, and 2016.

"There is a bigger pie in the sky that motivates us all as entrepreneurs," Pike said.

REFLECTION

Take the time to explore your financing options along the way like Pike has. Explore the different options and consider the pros and cons of each.

CASH FLOW, CASH FLOW, CASH FLOW

A critical consideration is what your monthly payment will be, which is based on the amortization of the loan and whether or not it is a revolver or a term loan. You have to be comfortable that the loan will work with your cash flow. As an example, it might make sense to pay a slightly higher rate in exchange for a longer amortization period and lower monthly payments.

Even entrepreneurs who are willing to take on debt tend to want to pay it off as soon as possible for fear the debt service will hang over their business like an omnipresent black cloud.

That's why they seek short amortization periods, often a year or less.

That may be a mistake.

You don't want excessive debt payments—if you can eliminate your debt in advance, more power to you.

Many businesses are cyclical, and even those that aren't cyclical have slow periods on occasion. At those times, an extended amortization period (and the resulting lower payments) can make your day-to-day business a lot more comfortable and eliminate the need for you to worry about lulls.

Long-term loans—with typical payback terms of three to ten years—often are better for more expensive or longer-term purchases.

It may be prudent to obtain a short-term loan to stock inventory before a busy period, make small equipment purchases, or to handle emergency repairs.

Long-term loans are best suited for things such as major equipment buys, real estate purchases, or acquiring another business. Do note that these loans are sometimes difficult to obtain, particularly for newer businesses that have shaky finances and/or lack a long track record.

There are other reasons why a longer amortization period makes sense.

For example, there's a strong possibility that you may hold other, high-interest short-term loans. Having a longer amortization period frees up cash flow that you can use to pay down the high-interest debt—or use for other pressing needs.

In the same vein, you might be able to use the money in a better way, such as by putting it in investments that will generate more cash for your business.

And while it hasn't been a big issue of late, if inflation is expected to rise long term, you'll want to borrow money at the lower rates because you'll be paying it back with dollars that are somewhat devalued.

Another issue with short-term loans is that they don't always stay that way. If cash flow runs tight and you can't make the payment, you might need to get another loan to make the first installment—a classic debt trap.

Short-term and long-term obligations have their places in business financing. By knowing how to make the best use of both of them, your odds of continued success will climb.

LINE OF CREDIT VS. TERM DEBT

When you need to borrow money for your business, the type of debt you take on makes a big difference. By matching up the right type of loan to your needs, you can coordinate the payments with your schedule and lower the amount you'll pay for financing.

To help you figure out what kind of loan to take out, I've presented some scenarios for which term debt is appropriate and some for which revolving debt is appropriate.

Term debt is a loan with a set payment schedule over several months or years. For example, say you borrow $50,000 and pay the money back with monthly payments over five years. These types of loans typically have a fixed interest rate with set payments, which makes them predictable. Usually, with term debt you can borrow higher amounts than you can with revolving debt. However, it takes more time to qualify for term debt, especially since each loan requires a new application.

Revolving debt has some significant differences. It's a loan with more flexibility about when you pay the money back—it's like a line of credit. After you set up your revolving loan, the lender tells you the maximum amount you can borrow. You can borrow money whenever you need it, pay it back on your schedule, then borrow again.

Revolving debt usually requires you to pay the money back quickly, and many revolvers require that you have a zero balance at some point each year, meaning you need to pay back everything you've borrowed. Otherwise, the lender could charge you a penalty or even shut down your revolving line of credit.

WHEN TO USE TERM DEBT

Term debt is appropriate for long-term investments in your business. These include projects like paying for renovations to your store or buying a new piece of machinery. These investments are one-time expenses whose launch schedule you choose. As a result, you can plan for the longer application process for term debt.

A term loan will also spread out the payments for these expenses, which can be relatively large. This will give you the time to pay off the investment over several years so your payments will be more manageable. Revolving debt doesn't match up well with these projects because you might not be able to borrow enough to pay for these significant expenses. You'll also likely borrow too much to pay it back quickly enough to meet the terms of revolving debt.

WHEN TO USE REVOLVING DEBT

Revolving debt is best used for your working-capital needs, like buying inventory, making payroll, or handling last-minute bills. These expenses are less predictable and come up more frequently. By having a revolver in place, you'll be able to borrow money quickly to pay off these expenses. Term debt has a longer application period, so it's typically too slow for these situations.

Since these expenses are also smaller, you should be able to pay them off more quickly, so you can handle the shorter window for paying off your revolving debt. You don't need the extra time from term debt.

The message here is: Don't burden your company with the wrong kind of financing. By keeping these general guidelines in mind, you can put together an effective debt plan for whatever expenses come your way.

CONSIDER THE SBA

The SBA is often not the first choice for business owners looking for financing, but the long-time lending giant has recently made significant changes that should bump it higher on your list when it comes to finding smart capital for your business.

The SBA is not a lender. It is a government guarantee program that encourages banks (and a handful of non-bank lenders) to take on riskier loans than they otherwise would. There are thousands of lenders in the country that utilize the program.

While every lender follows the same SBA rules, there are vast differences between them to be considered.

Every lender has their credit policy and criteria. A loan that is not appealing to one lender could be a home run for another one.

Furthermore, there are many different loan programs within the SBA. The lender whose branch you walk into might not utilize the loan program that is perfect for your business.

And finally, the person you are talking to at your bank (particularly if it's a bigger bank) might not know anything about SBA loans, even if the same bank has a department three floors up that specializes in them.

SBA loans can be an incredible tool to help you grow and expand your business at reasonable rates with an extended amortization. Be sure you speak to an expert who understands them, before ruling them out.

I won't dispute that the SBA has a reputation of being laboriously measured and overly bureaucratic, but then again, what government agency isn't? For business owners seeking quick capital, the turnaround times and legwork for an SBA loan are often prohibitive, even if the money is available at a lower rate and with more attractive terms than from its competitors. But the truth is, if you have the right lender working diligently and efficiently to pair you with the right SBA loan for your needs, the process can be as timely and painless as applying for a conventional loan.

Nonetheless, navigating the SBA loan process can be tricky even for experienced lenders. Business owners considering an SBA loan should do ample research into lenders that have experience (and good results) obtaining SBA loans for small businesses. If one lender tells you that you aren't a match for an SBA loan, seek a second opinion from a lender who may be more creative with solutions and experienced in dealing with the SBA's loan programs and their caveats and rules.

Over the years, our firm has had tremendous luck working with SBA lenders to create positive outcomes for our clients. In one example, we recently helped a trucking company obtain a $5 million SBA loan. They used the proceeds to refinance their building as well as about $2 million worth of their truck fleet. They were able to obtain a twenty-five-year amortization on the loan and improve their cash flow by hundreds of thousands of dollars a year, which was critical for a major new project they are undertaking.

If a business needs a dose of working capital, the SBA Express offers an appealing alternative. Many of our clients use this program to receive up to $350,000 on a ten-year amortization at a 7 percent interest rate—without the entrepreneur having to put up any personal collateral. This program has the benefit of allowing the business time to pay off their loan and maintain their cash flow.

The SBA has also made exceptional improvements to their CAPLINE program over the last several years. The CAPLINE program offers companies ABL facilities, often at dramatically cheaper rates than the private markets.

Whatever your situation is, don't rule out the SBA at the starting line. It might just be the perfect solution for your needs.

REFLECTION

What's the best way to shore up your balance sheet—taking on debt or offering equity to outside investors? Though I usually pick debt, it's important to consider the pros and cons of each.

Equity provides less personal risk, but it comes with lower reward as well because you're now splitting profits with someone else.

Taking on debt means higher risk and increased debt payments, but you usually retain more control over your company.

Which one feels right for you and your company?

Lending is a two-way relationship. Remember that investors expect to make money when they offer to finance your business. And don't fall into the trap of raising too much money. Think carefully before you leap.

The SBA can often help entrepreneurs find creative funding options. Have you made use of all resources available to you in your search for solutions to your growth dilemma?

PROFILE: CETRA LANGUAGE SOLUTIONS

For some entrepreneurs, the million-dollar question focuses on cash-flow issues.

One reason people become entrepreneurs is that they like the idea of controlling their own fate. That's why if Jiri Stejskal were given $1 million that he could divide between his business and a mutual fund, he would put 80 percent of it into CETRA Language Solutions, which is located just north of Philadelphia, in Elkins Park. "I'm in charge, so I can influence what the results can be. With the market, it's whether I get lucky or not, but I don't have any control over it," Stejskal said.

He would use the $800,000 to stabilize CETRA's cash flow and provide some wiggle room. He would like to shore up his balance sheet. It's a conservative use of the money that is often appropriate for many businesses.

Stejskal said he'd expect the fund to generate a return of less than 5 percent, while CETRA could potentially generate a return of more than 10 percent. At fifty-five, he sees himself owning and growing the company for at least the next five to ten years.

Stejskal started CETRA in 1997 while he was working on a PhD in Slavic languages and literatures at the University of Pennsylvania. Unisys, a computer company based in the northern

Philadelphia suburb of Blue Bell, was involved in a lawsuit with a Czech bank for which it was developing software.

While going through the discovery process, the law firm representing Unisys accumulated documents in Czech that it needed to have translated into English, so a law firm staff member called Penn's Slavic department for help and was put in touch with Stejskal. "I had to start a company overnight," he said.

Stejskal, who is of Czech origin, had been working with the American Translators Association at the time to organize a certification program for Czech languages, so he was well connected with the Czech translator community. He brought two people to Philadelphia to work with him and lined up about one hundred others to work as subcontractors, and CETRA was off and running.

Once introduced to the world of business, Stejskal was fascinated with it, so he continued running CETRA. And after he earned his PhD from Penn, he got an executive MBA from another Philadelphia school, Temple University.

Because it relied on contractors, CETRA didn't initially have much overhead, so it was profitable from its inception. "There's really no investment needed for this type of business," Stejskal said.

For a long time, all Stejskal had to do to keep CETRA growing was manage its cash flow. When he needed a little help with that, he turned to credit cards, and later secured a line of credit from his bank. Finally, in 2015, he secured a $100,000 loan to get more assistance with cash flow than could be provided by credit cards and the line of credit.

Stejskal said 75 percent of CETRA's work consists of document translation. Most of that is for market-research firms that work for Fortune 500 companies, doing such things as translating survey and opinion polls from English into multiple languages and repeating the process with poll and survey results. The company also provides translation services for other clients, including the US government.

By the beginning of 2015, CETRA had seven offices in five countries and was poised for future expansion, which was contingent on the company's revenue continuing to grow, which it didn't do in 2015. As a result, in addition to getting a $100,000 loan, the company had to cut costs in early 2016. It did, and Stejskal was expecting it to show a slight profit for the year on about $6 million in revenue. "We need to bring in more revenues to make it work better," he said.

Stejskal said that if he were given $1 million, the $800,000 he would put into CETRA would help with cash flow and provide more wiggle room in case of unforeseen challenges. The impact of the money would be significant because, when CETRA expands into other countries, its access to capital there is limited. Traditional US-based lenders are not interested in funding overseas expansion because they view it as too risky, and foreign banks either aren't lending or charge astronomical interest rates to subsidiaries of US companies.

Stejskal said that if he could borrow up to $1 million at 6 percent, he would borrow the entire amount to help CETRA grow. "I am confident the return would be better than the interest on the loan."

That confidence, plus how Stejskal would divide his hypothetical $1 million gift, makes him a grower.

REFLECTION

Stejskal is worried about cash flow. If you were in this boat, you wouldn't necessarily have to borrow through term debt, but you could consider a line of credit to help with cash flow ups and downs.

Do you have cash flow issues?

CHAPTER 10

Family Business/Partnerships

F amily businesses and partnerships can be complicated matters. It's important to work through the previous exercises with family business members and/or partners to see how your answers compare and where there might be tension. Let me explain more.

What does Harper Lee's classic novel *To Kill a Mockingbird*, which was turned into an equally stellar film, have to do with business? It gave us this quote: "You can choose your friends, but you sho' can't choose your family."

And although relatives are the bane of existence for some people, that doesn't stop many entrepreneurs from starting family-owned businesses—or entering into partnerships with close friends, who can be just as frustrating as relatives.

Let's look at the pros and cons of a business with principals who have close ties. On the plus side, loyalty should be strong and the goals are likely to be similar.

As the *Houston Chronicle* noted on its website, chron.com, "Having a certain level of intimacy among the owners of a business can help bring about familiarity with the company and having family members around provides a built-in support system that should ensure teamwork and solidarity. Other benefits of a family business include long-term stability, trust, loyalty and shared values."[1]

Don't forget stability: Family members are far more likely to stick in there with you in the long run than outsiders who might bolt the first time a better opportunity presents itself.

In addition, family members are more likely to be flexible. Need to take your child to the doctor or soccer practice? Want to take a long weekend on your anniversary? Family members are probably going to be more understanding than strangers.

It should be noted that family-owned businesses seem to enjoy extra cachet among customers; the personal touch appeals to customers, suppliers, and circles of influence.

And a family-run business tends to have lower starting costs because participants may well work for free or for little compensation until things get up and running.

Moving to the negative side, just because someone is a relative doesn't mean they are right for the company. And because they're family, it will be that much harder to remove them from the job

---

1   Alexis Writing, "Pros & Cons of Family Business," *Chron*, August 5, 2017, http://smallbusiness.chron.com/pros-cons-family-business-409.html.

if they prove to be inadequate. Balancing business needs with personal relationships can be tricky.

Meanwhile, sibling rivalries may rear their ugly heads. And differences regarding succession—what happens when the next generation has radically different ideas or simply isn't interested in the business?—may also wreak havoc both in the business and in your personal life.

Because everyone's related (or at least the key members are), a clear corporate structure may well be lacking, which can lead to regulatory issues and poor professionalism. Employees who aren't part of the family may feel resentful and neglected, especially when nepotism is obvious.

Also consider that a family business may lack proper perspective and alternative viewpoints. If everyone working in the business has similar life experiences, they're also likely to have the same blind spots. Group thinking in this case won't be helpful.

That leads to this question: What can be done to prevent problems and reduce the risks—there's no way to completely eliminate them—faced by family businesses and close partnerships?

Consider the previously discussed risk tolerance exercise.

Have each potential partner take the test, then compare answers. This will give you a compatibility gauge in terms of business philosophy.

If you score as risk flexible but brother Tom is risk neutral and cousin Joe is risk averse, you're going to clash. Conversely, if your scores are similar, you might expect reasonably good compatibility, which bodes well for your working relationships.

In addition, have everyone complete the chapter on stretch

goals. Granted, it's a bit premature if your business isn't underway, but your answers provide another information point for comparing business philosophies. If partners have dramatically different perspectives on how quickly the business should grow, tensions can arise.

Plenty of family-owned businesses exist in the world today, and there's no inherent reason to dismiss the idea out of hand. That said, compatibility may well be the ultimate deciding factor in success, so be sure to consider working relationships before moving forward.

REFLECTION

There are pros and cons to staying in a family-run or partner business. Pros: loyalty, trust, stability, familiarity. Cons: incompatibility, old sibling rivalries, divergent goals, dissimilar risk-tolerance levels.

How compatible are you and your partners?

PROFILE: MULTIFUNDING

As a finale, I thought I would share my approaches to the growth dilemma during different stages of the life of my company, MultiFunding. I hope these personal insights will give you more food for thought.

Many people don't know that I started MultiFunding with a partner. We each put in $7,500 and naïvely thought that would be enough to get going. Before we started, we had no serious discussions about how much money we expected it would take to get up and running, what risks we were each willing to take, and what each of us expected of our company.

Just a few short months after we started, my partner announced that he wanted to move back to his home in Austria. While at the time it felt as though his decision was the end of the world for the company, in retrospect it was, perhaps, the best thing that could have happened.

I can't be certain, but I don't think he would have seen eye to eye with me as we tried to build the company. He was single and much younger than I was. I had a wife, a mortgage, and two kids.

I have received way too many phone calls over the years about partnerships that have gone sour. My business partnership was relatively easy to clean up, as we had nothing going yet. It was like a divorce without kids. Most breakups are tougher than ours was. If you're going to build a business with partners, I encourage you to have long and hard conversations about money, risk, and time horizons.

In the first few years, I tried to build the business purely off of cash flow. I wanted to do it on my own and not take on investors. It was tougher and harder than I expected. And perhaps it was the wrong decision. I watched our savings dwindle away as I obstinately went about the business my way.

You often hear stories about how it's longer and harder and tougher to build a business than you could anticipate. The problem is that you don't think this rule of thumb applies to you. But then you get in the game of cash-flow roulette, and you learn survival skills that they don't teach you in business school.

As I fought through this struggle, I watched friends raise hundreds of millions of dollars for their fin-tech companies. And while I knew risk was inherent in their approach, I have to tell you I was tempted more than once to jump onto what I call the venture-capital treadmill. Sometimes I felt foolish being so small and living on such a tight budget and lying awake at night worrying about how I was going to make payroll next Wednesday.

This is the inherent tension between the tortoise or hare approach to entrepreneurship.

I will never forget the day when I was sitting in the offices of one of those fin-tech companies in San Francisco. Its monthly rent was probably our annual payroll. Suddenly, someone rang a big bell. I thought to myself, "Wow—they must have just closed a loan." They were actually celebrating their next hire. Their team was up to eighty-seven, and they were just getting started. At that point, we had eight people in all.

Ironically, many of the companies that chose the hare approach that I once longed for are now struggling and facing massive losses. Meanwhile, at my company, we are finally hitting our stride and finding a formula that works.

I don't offer this story up to gloat or suggest that I won and they lost. It is important because it presents examples of the contrasting financing choices entrepreneurs can make.

As I worked through the process of trying to grow my company, I eventually hit a point where I was out of savings and lacked the ability to borrow. I was lucky and fortunate enough to take on an investor who had the same philosophy about growing a company as I did. He was willing to put in small amounts of cash as we needed it as we worked to figure out our formula.

Investors can be a mixed blessing. Think about an investor in the same way you would a partner; it's a marriage, whether you like it or not. Interview each other well before you jump into a decision.

Our company has recently hit a stride of growth and healthy cash flow. It feels great. And part of me would like to relax and enjoy it.

Now let me answer the million-dollar question I put to other entrepreneurs.

If I had an extra $1 million, I would likely take about $300,000 and stash it away somewhere for a rainy day. I would sleep better at night because I have poured everything into the company.

But then I would take the extra $700,000 and invest it in building a national sales/advisory team for our business. It's the next logical step, and I know we need it. Now I should pluck up the courage to *Just Do It*, as the slogan goes, and figure out how to finance such a move.

But then again, perhaps I am like the shoemaker without soles on his shoes.

Finding Your Financing Comfort Zone

I hope this book has given you the opportunity to think through your attitudes about finance and risk and how they impact your entrepreneurial journey. Consider taking a few minutes to answer some of the key questions this book has posed, to help you understand the choices you are making and where you fit into the ecosystem. Remember that there are no right or wrong answers; these are personal and difficult choices.

A lot of information has come your way as you've read these pages, so now it's time for a little self-diagnosis. Using the tools provided, you should be able to get a snapshot of what is holding you back from growing your business and whether you want to make any changes accordingly.

Remember that this snapshot is a moment in time: Things change—often quickly—so feel free to repeat this exercise as needed. In fact, you probably should incorporate regular status checks into your planning.

ARE YOU A 100 PERCENTER OR A SAFETY NETTER?

The heart of this book is the entrepreneur profiles. Remember that each entrepreneur was asked how they would divide a hypothetical $1 million gift when given the option of investing it in their business or stashing it in a mutual fund. A second question changed the parameters a bit, making the $1 million a loan at 6 percent interest instead of a gift.

It probably doesn't surprise you that a majority of the people profiled chose to invest all (or most) of the money into their businesses. After all, entrepreneurs tend to be self-confident about both themselves and their businesses.

What would you do?

We're almost done, but there are two more things to consider: whether you're a tortoise or a hare and whether you prefer debt or equity financing. The two topics go together.

TORTOISE VS. HARE

If you're a tortoise, you prefer gradual growth over an extended period of time. Rome wasn't built in a day—and the same is true of your business. That's why you'd probably prefer debt financing, which tends to be less risky and keeps control of the company in your hands.

That's the preferred path recommended for most clients.

But perhaps you're not "most clients." Maybe you know that the time to strike is now—that there's a huge opportunity awaiting your business that you can't miss.

That makes you a hare. It also means you need a ready source of money, also known as equity financing. That could come from angel investors, private equity, venture capitalists, and so on.

You may get your money, but giving up part of your ownership can have pitfalls, especially if your investors have different ideas and goals than you do.

WHERE ARE YOU IN YOUR BUSINESS JOURNEY?

The first thing to puzzle out is the current stage of your business journey.

Are you a grower, looking to expand your business—probably in a rapid manner? If so, it's an exciting time for you and, to quote a cliché, the world is your oyster.

Or perhaps you've been in business for a while and things are going well. You're enjoying steady growth and have an established niche in your market. If so, you are among the gliders and are not looking to make major changes, although you'd consider it if the right opportunity came along.

Perhaps you've hit a rough patch, which makes you a speed-bumper. Examples of those speed-bumps might include the departure of a key executive or a sharp increase in the price of raw materials that makes your product less cost-competitive in the marketplace. Or perhaps a competitor has come up with something that's simply better than what you offer. Sometimes these problems can be overcome, but sometimes they can't.

Finally, does the idea of time on the golf course, on your boat, or simply playing with your grandkids now seem more appealing than continuing your business? If so, you're an exiter.

WHAT IS YOUR RISK TOLERANCE?

Now that you've clarified where things stand, review your risk tolerance. There are no right or wrong answers; entrepreneurs have very different reactions when it comes to risk.

Complete the survey on p.74 and see where you stand. Those who are risk flexible will have more options available to them than the risk neutral and, especially, the risk averse—although remember, there are always options.

WHAT IS YOUR GROWTH ASPIRATION?

For more insight into yourself, consider your stretch goals—and complete the questionnaire that begins on p.89.

While you might think this is simply asking about risk tolerance again, it's more a method for fine-tuning your thinking about both lending and your business.

The definition of a stretch goal bears repeating: A stretch goal is something that goes a bit beyond what a business might consider a reasonable expectation. Stretch goals are challenging, but they're not beyond the realm of possibility, either.

Do you consider yourself a conservative stretcher, a rocket-ship stretcher, or something in the middle?

While reputable lenders won't steer you toward anything that makes you uncomfortable, discomfort can be useful for you to look beyond your limits, if only slightly. Given the many funding options out there—options you may never have considered—stretch goals often are easier to achieve than they might appear.

By now, you should have a solid feel for what you need, but consider a few more things.

A FINAL REFLECTION

The questions in this book are deep and personal. I hope this book and the stories inside it have stirred your thinking about your business, your growth dilemma, and your financing comfort zone. And whatever the outcome is for you, I wish you an inspiring entrepreneurial adventure.

Remember that this is a journey. It's striking to me that how I answer some of these questions today would have been different a year ago. And in a year, they will likely change again.

So, my last challenge to you is to make a note in your calendar to flip through this book again a year from now. Your evolution in thinking might surprise you.

AN ADDITIONAL RESOURCE

To help you as you continue on your journey, www.growthdilemma.com offers you a customized Growth Dilemma report. Once you're on the site, click the button on the top right corner of the home page to start your personalized assessment.

Acknowledgments

I once heard the saying, "It takes a village to raise a child." I think it's also fair to say, "It takes a village to write a book."

I want to thank the fifteen entrepreneurs who were profiled in this book and generous enough to share their time and insights with us.

Many people read the manuscript at various points along the way. I want to thank David Nast, Dennis Alter, Chuck Andrews, Tripp David, Arnie Fishman, Andrew Geisler, John Loftus, Lonnie Martin, and Jim Twerdahl.

Thank you to Eric Schurenberg and his team at *Inc.* magazine for providing me with a creative platform on which to share my writing. A particular thanks to Patrick Hainult from *Inc.* who pushed me to use the Greenleaf Book Group to publish this book. They made a vast difference.

A few other important mentions.

Thanks to Loren Feldman at *Forbes* who sent me kicking and screaming into blogging for *The New York Times* many years ago. That beginning was an important step into this adventure.

I want to thank the Vistage community; I have been honored to work with and learn from the chairs and members of the community. Their insights have helped me fine-tune many of the ideas in this book.

Thank you to Andy Gotlieb and Peter Key for helping me with a lot of the research and interviewing for this book.

And thanks go to the entire MultiFunding team, including Kate Stackhouse, Irish Olynyk, Daniel Krewson, Fran Miller, Heather Hoover, Karin Fortier, and many others whose dedication to their work is second to none.

And finally, thanks to my wife, Bethany, and our kids, Sam and Charlotte, who put up with the erratic schedule and work/life balance of a perpetual grower.

Index

A

ABL (asset-based lending), 127
aggressive stretchers, 93
Amazon.com, 43, 65, 95
American Express OPEN Small
    Business Growth Pulse survey,
    47–48
American Fire Glass, 53–54,
    61–64
American Translators Association,
    129
amortization, 121–22
    base scenario, 102
    best-case scenario, 103
    worst-case scenario, 100
Amusement Today, 120
angel investors, 44, 112, 143
Artists Frame Service, 23–25, 54
asset-based lending (ABL), 127
Association Headquarters, 20–22,
    25, 52

B

Bamberger's, 66
bankability
    million-dollar question, 117–18
    path to, 116
    Skyline Attractions profile,
    117–20

Bank of America Merrill Lynch, 42
BD Capital Partners LLC, 46
Bella + Prisma, 24
benefitRFP, 45–47, 52
Berkley, Gladys, 27
borrowing. *See* financing
Boyce, Jason, 94–96
Brown, Paul B., 77
business guarantees, 80

C

California Outdoor Concepts,
    63–64
CAPLINE program, 127
cash flow, 11, 24, 121–22
    base scenario, 101–2
    best-case scenario, 102–3
    as bottleneck, 62
    CETRA Language Solutions
    profile, 128–32
    debt financing, 113
    leverage, 97–98
    million-dollar question, 128,
    130
    return on investment, 104–6
    risk tolerance levels, 78
    SBA loans, 126–27
    worst-case scenario, 100

CETRA Language Solutions, 128–32
Chicago Art Source, 24
Christine Taylor Collection, 65–68
Cino, Nadine, 40–43, 52
ClickAway, 58–60
collateral, 72–73, 110, 113
   hare entrepreneurs, 44
   leverage, 97
   risk tolerance levels, 75, 77–78, 80
conservative stretchers, 92
Cooperberg, David, 27–29, 53
'corePHP,' 13–15, 52

D
Danish, Matt, 55–57
Dazadi, 94–96
debt financing
   pros and cons of, 113
   tortoise entrepreneurs, 38–39, 48, 143
Doll, Matt, 54, 61–64
Dwyer, Michael, 20–22, 25, 52

E
EBITDA (earnings before interest, taxes, depreciation, and amortization), 88, 90–91
Entrepreneurship for the Rest of Us (Brown), 77
equity financing
   cautions regarding, 111
   hare entrepreneurs, 44, 48, 143
   pros and cons of, 112
   scenarios favoring, 111
EuropaPark, 120
exiters, 65–68, 144

Artists Frame Service profile, 23–25
Christine Taylor Collection profile, 65–68
defined, 54
million-dollar question, 65, 68

F
factoring, 72–73, 115
   bankability, 38-39, 116–20
family businesses and partnerships, 133–40
   advantages of, 134
   disadvantages of, 134–35
   MultiFunding profile, 137–40
   risk tolerance levels, 135
   stretch goals, 135–36
FDIC, 116
financing, 2–3, 95. *See also* million-dollar question
   base scenario, 98, 101–2, 105–6
   best-case scenario, 98, 102–3
   cash flow, 121–22, 128–32
   debt financing, 38–39, 48, 113, 143
   equity financing, 44, 48, 111–12, 143
   "fighting gravity," 114–15
   loan application mistakes, 110
   raising too much money, 110
   return on investment, 104–6
   reviewing loans annually, 114
   revolving debt vs. term debt, 123–25
   SBA loans, 125–27
   short-term vs. long-term loans, 121–22

Skyline Attractions profile, 117–20
two-way relationship of lending,
114–15
worst-case scenario, 98–101,
104–6
financing comfort zone, viii,
141–46
challenging assumptions, 4
lifecycle stages, 51–52
million-dollar question, 9
FishPreneurs story, vii–viii
floor-plan lines of credit, 115
Forbes, 23, 77, 91, 150

G

gliders, 53, 58–60, 144
ClickAway profile, 58–60
Imacuclean profile, 27–29
million-dollar question, 53,
58–60
Goltz, Jay, 23–25, 54
Gray, Chris, 118–19
Great Coasters International, 117,
119
The Great Game of Business (Stack),
85
growers, 52, 55–57, 131, 144
Association Headquarters profile, 20–22, 25
benefitRFP profile, 45–47
'corePHP' profile, 13–15
million-dollar question, 52,
56–57
pros and cons of, 52
Telex Metals profile, 55–57
Tyga-Box Systems profile,
40–43

Unique Indoor Comfort profile,
34–36
growth aspirations, 7, 87–96,
145–46
aggressive stretchers, 93
conservative stretchers, 92
debt as option for funding,
88–89
moderate stretchers, 92
reachability of, 91–92
rocket-ship stretchers, 93–96
worksheet for identifying,
89–90
growth dilemma
base scenario, 98, 101–2, 105–6
best-case scenario, 98, 102–3
defined, vii, 31–32
difficulty in identifying next
step, 3–4
fear of risk in borrowing, 33
FishPreneurs story, vii–viii
overleveraged vs. underleveraged, 97–98
raising or borrowing money as
crutch, 32
Unique Indoor Comfort profile,
34–36
worst-case scenario, 98–101,
104–6
Growth Dilemma report website,
7, 147
Guardian, 45
Gurule, John, 56

H

hare entrepreneurs, 37, 44–49, 143
benefitRFP profile, 45–47

choosing between approaches,
47–49
defined, 5, 44, 48
equity financing, 44
Harth, Allyn, 84
Harth, Gregory, 84–86
Holiday World, 119
home-equity lines of credit (HE-
LOCs), 2, 39, 78
home-equity loans, 78
home liens, 11–12, 70, 80
Houston Chronicle, 134

I

Imacuclean, 27–29, 53
Individual Retirement Accounts
(IRAs), 78
insurance
borrowing against, 78
FDIC, 116
personal guarantee, 71
International Association of
Amusement Parks and Attrac-
tions, 118
IRAs (Individual Retirement Ac-
counts), 78

J

Jayson Home, 24
Johnson & Johnson, 34
Joomla!, 13

K

Kassar, Ami, vii, xii, 1–3, 137–40,
151-2
Kukla, Nate, 33–36, 52

L

Lee, Harper, 133
leverage, 33, 104–6
overleveraged vs. underleveraged, 97–98
risk tolerance levels, 76
liens, 71–73
on home, 11–12, 70, 80
subordinate positions, 71–72
lifecycle stages, 6, 51–68, 144
exiters, 54, 65–68, 144
gliders, 53, 58–60, 144
growers, 52, 55–57, 144
speed-bumpers, 53–54, 61–64,
144
loans. *See* financing

M

Mack family, 120
MacMillan, Bill, 20–21
Macy's, 66
Maguire, Jim, 56
Mambo, 13
million-dollar question, 4, 9–15
age and length of time in business, 40, 43
American Fire Glass profile,
61–62
Artists Frame Service profile,
23, 25
Association Headquarters profile, 20–22, 25
bankability, 117–18
cash flow, 128, 130
CETRA Language Solutions
profile, 128, 130

Christine Taylor Collection
  profile, 65, 68
ClickAway profile, 58–60
'corePHP' profile, 13–15
Dazadi profile, 94–95
emotional component, 11–12
entrepreneurs that can't answer,
  27, 29
exiters, 65, 68
gliders, 53, 58–60
growers, 52, 56–57
Harth Builders profile, 84, 86
Imacuclean profile, 27, 29
importance of, 11
methodical formula for deciding, 14–15
MultiFunding profile, 139
100 percenters, 17, 20–22, 25,
  33–36
risk-averse entrepreneurs, 84, 86
rocket-ship stretchers, 94–95
safety netters, 17–18, 23, 25
Skyline Attractions profile,
  117–18
speed-bumpers, 53, 61–62
Telex Metals profile, 56–57
Tyga-Box Systems profile, 40,
  43
Unique Indoor Comfort profile,
  33–36
what your answer reveals, 9–10
worksheet for, 10
Minor Metals Trade Association
  (MMTA), 55–57
moderate stretchers, 92
MultiFunding, 2–3, 137–40,
  150-2

Mutz, Frank, 34

N
Nass, Steffen, 46
Neiman Marcus, 67
Nienaber, Bob, 45–47, 52
no-debt entrepreneurs, 33, 81–82

O
100 percenters, 17–18, 20–22,
  25–29, 142
  appeal of, 18
  Association Headquarters pro-
    file, 20–22, 25
  defined, 17
  Imacuclean profile, 27–29
Open-Book Management process,
  85

P
paGO Commerce, 14–15
personal guarantees, 70–71, 74,
  77–78, 80
Philadelphia Business Journal, 85
Phoenix Companies of America,
  45
PHP programming language, 13
Pignataro, Michael, 13–15, 52
Pignataro, Steven, 13–14
Pike, Jeff, 117–19
Principal Financial Group, 45
private equity, 44, 143
Procter & Gamble, 43
profiles
  American Fire Glass, 61–64
  Artists Frame Service, 23–25
  Association Headquarters,
    20–22

benefitRFP, 45–47
CETRA Language Solutions, 128–32
Christine Taylor Collection, 65–68
ClickAway, 58–60
'corePHP,' 13–15
Dazadi, 94–96
Harth Builders, 84–86
Imacuclean, 27–29
MultiFunding, 137–40
Skyline Attractions, 117–20
Telex Metals, 55–57
Tyga-Box Systems, 40–43
Unique Indoor Comfort, 34–36

R

return on investment (ROI), 104–6
base scenario, 101–2
best-case scenario, 102–3
worst-case scenario, 100
revolving debt
defined, 123
when to use, 124–25
risk-averse entrepreneurs, 76–78, 84–86
defined, 76–77
Harth Builders profile, 84–86
million-dollar question, 84, 86
options for, 77–78
risk-neutral vs., 79
risk-flexible entrepreneurs, 76, 79–80
defined, 76, 79
risk-neutral entrepreneurs, 76, 78–79

defined, 76, 78
risk-averse vs., 79
risk tolerance levels, 6, 69–86, 145
family businesses and partnerships, 135
loan document terminology, 70–73
no-debt entrepreneurs, 81–82
100 percenters vs. safety netters, 18
questionnaire for determining, 74–76
risk-averse entrepreneurs, 76–78, 84–86
risk-flexible entrepreneurs, 76, 79–80
risk-neutral entrepreneurs, 76, 78–79
Rocket-Ship Stretchers
Dazadi profile, 94–96
defined, 93
million-dollar question, 94–95
ROI. *See* return on investment

S

safety netters, 17–19, 23–29, 142
Artists Frame Service profile, 23–25
defined, 17
Imacuclean profile, 27–29
sound reasons for caution, 18–19
Sageworks, 91
SBA (Small Business Administration) loans, 11, 24, 73, 99, 113, 125–27

American Fire Glass profile, 62–63
  bankability, 116
  CAPLINE program, 127
  personal guarantees, 70
  risk-averse entrepreneurs, 78
  SBA Express program, 126–27
  stretch goals, 88
  Tyga-Box Systems profile, 42
Six Flags over Georgia, 119
Skyline Attractions, 117–20
Souliere, Evan, 118–19
speed-bumpers, 53–54, 61–64,
  144
  American Fire Glass profile,
  61–64
  million-dollar question, 53,
  61–62
Spindel, Marty, 40–41
Stack, Jack, 85
Stejskal, Jiri, 128–29
The Street-Smart Entrepreneur
  (Goltz), 23
stretch goals, 87–96
  aggressive stretchers, 93
  conservative stretchers, 92
  Dazadi profile, 94–96
  debt as option for funding,
  88–89
  defined, 87, 145
  family businesses and partnerships, 135–36
  moderate stretchers, 92
  obstacles, 89–90
  reachability of, 91–92
  rocket-ship stretchers, 93–96
  types of stretchers, 92–93
  worksheet for identifying,
  89–90

Sutherland, Rick, 58–60

T
Taylor, Christine, 65–68
Telex Metals, 55–57
term debt
  defined, 123
  when to use, 124
To Kill a Mockingbird (Lee), 133
tortoise entrepreneurs, 37–43,
  47–49, 143
  choosing between approaches,
  47–49
  debt financing considerations,
  38–39
  defined, 5, 38, 48
  Tyga-Box Systems profile,
  40–43
TripAdvisor, 120
Tyga-Box Systems, 40–43, 52

U
unicorns, 44
Unique Indoor Comfort, 34–36,
  52
Unisys, 128–29

V
venture capital, 25, 44, 112, 138,
  143
Verizon Wireless, 59

W
Waller, Bob, 20–21
Walmart, 95
Wayfair, 95
Welgs, Lara, 56
Wydra, Bill, 118–19

About the Author

Ami Kassar is the founder and CEO of MultiFunding LLC. He is a nationally renowned expert on access to capital for entrepreneurs. He's committed to ensuring that business owners have the best possible access to the capital structures they need to help grow and manage their businesses.

Kassar is regularly featured in the national press and writes a regular column for Inc.com. He has advised the White House, the Federal Reserve Bank, and the Treasury Department on the business credit markets. In addition, Kassar is a regular speaker at trade shows and business events across the country on topics including entrepreneurship and access to capital.

He is the 2015, 2014, and 2013 recipient of the Small Business Influencer Award as well as the 2012 Small Business Advocate

Award. Kassar earned his MBA from the University of Southern California and graduated with a BA in American Studies from Brandeis University.

Kassar's company, MultiFunding, has helped over seven hundred entrepreneurs across America raise over $300 million of capital for their businesses.

Kassar lives in the suburbs of Philadelphia with his wife, two kids, and two dogs.

91438433R00107

Made in the USA
Columbia, SC
15 March 2018